From First Kiss to Forever:

A Scientific Approach to Love

Marisa T. Cohen, Ph.D.

Published by Open Books

Copyright © 2016 by Marisa T. Cohen

All rights reserved. No part of this book may be reproduced, scanned, or distributed in any printed or electronic form without permission except in the case of brief quotations embodied in critical articles and reviews.

ISBN-10: 0997806265/ISBN-13: 978-0997806267

"Because here is perhaps the most important thing I learned: Love is not (entirely) unknowable. We'll never unravel all its mysteries, of course, nor would we want to. But we can get better at and smart about it, and increase our chances of creating happy, fulfilling relationships. We just have to be willing to listen to those who've come before us."

—Ellen McCarthy, *The Real Thing: Lessons on Love and Life from A Wedding Reporter's Notebook*

To those who I love and to those who love me.
Thank you.

TABLE OF CONTENTS

I.	What Is Love and Why Do We Care? An Introduction	5
	1. Introduction and Focus	7
II.	What I Like About You: Meeting Your Ideal Match	11
	1. Creating Closeness in the Lab and in Real Life	13
	2. "Clicking" with Online Dating	17
III.	It's Not You, It's Me: The Art and Science of Mate Choice	21
	1. Finding Your Needle in the Haystack	23
	2. More Choices, More Problems	27
IV.	It's Something in the Way He/She Looks: Features and Physical Attraction	31
	1. Features that Signal Attractiveness: The Kylie Jenner Effect	33
	2. From Bratz® to Natural Beauties	37
V.	War of the Sexes: Gender Differences in Dating and Relationships	41
	1. Do Women Have to Downplay Their Intelligence to Secure a Date?	43
	2. First Date Interactions: Does Gender Play a Role?	47

VI.	**Actions are Worth More than Words: Expressing Love for Your Partner**	**53**
	1. Giving the Gift of an Experience this Valentine's Day	55
	2. Playing Hard to Get Potentially Fried this Frog	59
VII.	**Understanding our Bodies: The Role of Physiological Arousal and Emotions**	**63**
	1. Misattribution in Paradise	65
	2. Why Do We Watch Romantic Movies During Winter Storms?	69
VIII.	**The Design of Love: Relationship Structure and Configurations**	**73**
	1. Is Marriage Really Synonymous with Monogamy?	75
	2. Polyamory: Understanding Relationship Geometry	79
IX.	**When the Past Influences Our Present and Future: Thinking About Ex-Partners**	**85**
	1. The Ghost of Relationships Past	87
	2. How a White Bear Can Teach You to Forget Your Ex	91
	3. Breaking Up Is Hard to Do	95

X.	**The Dark Side: Infidelity in Relationships**	**99**
	1. A "Double-Shot" of Cheating	101
	2. Infidelity and Jealousy from an Evolutionary Perspective	105
XI.	**Steps for Success: Keys for Long, Lasting, and Loving Relationships**	**111**
	1. Combating the Four Horsemen	113
	2. The Shape of Love and Filling Our Tank	117
XII.	**The Power of Love: Concluding Thoughts and Final Remarks**	**121**
	1. Conclusion	123
XIII.	**Footnotes**	**125**
XIV.	**References**	**135**
XV.	**Appendix A**	**145**
	MateMatch Questions	147
	MateMatch References	155
XVI.	**Acknowledgements**	**159**

I. What Is Love and Why Do We Care? An Introduction

1. Introduction and Focus

Belongingness is a basic human need, and as a result, we have a pervasive desire to form and maintain long-lasting and positive relationships.[1] Relationships, whether they are friendships, family associations, or romantic connections, are important for our well-being, and their initiation is associated with happiness, elation, love, and joy. Researchers have also shown that marriage can boost self-esteem and lead to an overall positive sense of self, as married individuals report greater subjective well-being than persons who were never married, divorced, separated or widowed.[2] Beyond the emotional benefits, marital relationships also serve as buffers against stress,[3] and stronger marital quality is associated with better health.[4,5]

Most research designated to highlight the benefits that result from social bonds focuses on marriage. However, recent literature has extended the benefits derived by those in marriages to people in stable relationships. Research has shown that individuals in romantic relationships report more happiness than those who are not.[6,7]

Maybe it is due to the emotional benefits conferred by relationships, or maybe it is our natural curiosity, but we as humans have a desire to understand how love operates, the tricks to finding and securing our ideal match, and the secrets to making a relationship survive and thrive. A simple search on Amazon for love and/or dating books will garner well over 100,000 hits. It seems that we have a fascination with this complex emotion.

So who am I, and why have I decided to delve into the science of love? I am a psychology professor at a small private college in Brooklyn, New York with a background in educational psychology. My research focus originally began with an examination of learning and how to self-assess our knowledge. However, as a result of my relationship experiences and those of my friends, my focus shifted. I now investigate relationship-related behaviors and how people bond with one another.

I have incorporated my newfound interest in love with my previous education-based research. This led to an initial interdisciplinary study that sought to examine the importance of a person's educational background when selecting a potential mate. I also developed some interesting and interactive course material, which helped with the formation of what turned out to be a popular seminar class on attraction and attachment. After working with very dedicated students on research for this course, I felt inspired to create a lab based on the science of relationships. It is through this lab, and our projects, that our questions about love are answered, and new areas of interest and research are sparked.

As I mentioned earlier, I teach an attachment and attraction seminar each spring semester. I always begin the first class with a question that has often been posed to me, "What is love?" Invariably, the class laughs at the idea of answering such a general and yet simple question. I mean, we have all experienced love at some point in our lives, whether in relation to our family, our friends, or our partners. After a few moments of silence, and without a single pen lifted to their papers, I always notice that the students' expressions shift from that of elation to one of utter confusion.

How can this complex construct be adequately defined? They often struggle for several minutes before managing to write something down. I have received answers ranging from the description of infatuation to long-term companionate love, to a resounding, "there is no such thing as love."

After several semesters of this fun, yet challenging activity, I have gathered a wealth of information:

- Love is biological- it is hormones, anatomy, and the brain.
- Love is an emotion- it is pleasure, pain, euphoria, and fear.
- Love is reciprocated, unrequited, long awaited, and unexpected.
- Love is making that first move, saying "I do," and knowing when to walk away.
- Love is friendship, dating, intimacy, and sex.
- Love is powerful, all-consuming, terrifying and sometimes simply not enough.
- Love is a spike in oxytocin, sweaty palms, and "butterflies in the stomach" sensations.
- Love is your caregiver, your partner, your friend, or your foe.
- Love is exciting, nerve-racking, comforting, and distracting.
- Love is a hashtag, a punchline, a fairy tale, and a goal.
- Love is amazing, sensational, hard to define, and currently ours to explore.

The following chapters present discussions of various relationship-related topics, all backed by, and grounded in scientific principles and research. These chapters create a narrative, ranging from finding your match, to the birth of a relationship, to the achievement of a fulfilling partnership.

As you read, I challenge you to think of your own relationships and how they are similar to/different from those described in the text. This book will provide you with some take-home points/questions to address at the end of each section, as applying relationship science to everyday life is an important goal for this project.

As you examine these chapters and tips, I wish you a wealth of new knowledge, inspiration for strengthening your existing relationships, and a whole lot of love.

II. What I Like About You: Meeting Your Ideal Match

1. Creating Closeness in the Lab and in Real Life

Closeness in Real Life

During the weeks leading up to Valentine's Day 2015, social media feeds were flooded with Mandy Len Catron's (2015) *New York Times* article[1] discussing Arthur Aron's (1997) study, which was aimed at creating interpersonal closeness. The article focused on a series of questions that involved increasing levels of self-disclosure, which helped develop intimacy between people. Shortly following the publication of this article, peoples' accounts of their own experiences with Aron et al.'s 36 questions, spread all over social media.

Ms. Catron put social psychologist Arthur Aron's questions to the test by spending 90 minutes answering them in a bar with a university acquaintance of hers and then by standing on a bridge, staring into this man's eyes. Before describing the outcome of her real life research replication, it is important to outline Aron et al.'s work.

Closeness in the Lab

In the Aron et al. (1997) experiment,[2] pairs of individuals, over the course of 45 minutes, carried out self-disclosure and relationship-building tasks that gradually increased in intensity. A common misconception is that the goal was to create a long-lasting relationship between the individuals in the study, but rather the researchers sought to create a temporary feeling of closeness.

In the first part of the experiment, individuals were put into pairs, based on their attachment styles and attitudes. Pairs were given envelopes and told that they would be participating in a relationship-building exercise. They were randomly assigned either to complete tasks that involved self-disclosure or to engage in small talk. A sample small talk question was, "If you could invent a new flavor of ice cream, what would it be?" Those in the self-disclosure task were presented with questions such as, "What would constitute a 'perfect' day for you?" As you can see, the self-disclosure task required the individual to really think about him/herself as a person, and potentially to reveal important, intimate information to the partner. Those in the self-disclosure condition reported feeling closer to their partners after the study.

In the second study, the researchers followed the same procedure, but they added additional manipulations. The first manipulation was that participants were matched to partners who did not disagree on any attitudinal items that were important to them. The second manipulation was that the participants either expected mutual liking (they were told that they were carefully matched) or did not expect mutual liking (they were told that random matches were made). Attitudinal similarity and the expectation of the participants' liking one another did not help them achieve greater closeness than in the previous study. This may have been because the relationship-building tasks were so powerful that none of these additional steps even mattered.

In the final study, closeness was an explicit task. Specifically, participants were matched based on how introverted or extroverted they were. In one condition, researchers explained that the goal was for them to get close to their partner, while in the other condition, they were merely told to follow the directions. The extroverted pairs reported becoming closer to each other in the follow the directions condition (compared to the introverted couples), but a major difference was not seen in the "closeness-as-task" condition.

Overall, these studies demonstrated that, in fact, people found themselves closer after the self-disclosure tasks than others who merely engaged in regular small talk. In studies 2 and 3, no differences were found between whether or not pairs were matched based on similarity of attitudes, the expectation that the partner would like him/her, or whether or not the goal to become close was made explicit.

Back to the Real World

Now Mandy Len Catron tried this in a bar, not in a laboratory setting, with a person she already knew. Over the period of two hours, during which she and her partner answered the questions, she reported feeling an increased level of intimacy. After finishing the questions, she and her university acquaintance decided to try staring into each other's eyes for a period of four minutes. This eye gazing technique is a manipulation that has been used in Aron's other studies.

Ms. Catron ends the article by saying, "You're probably wondering if he and I fell in love. Well, we did. Although it's hard to credit the study entirely (it may have happened anyway), the study did give us a way into a relationship that feels deliberate. We spent weeks in the intimate space we created that night, waiting to see what it could become. Love didn't happen to us. We're in love because we each made the choice to be."[1]

TAKE HOME TIPS/QUESTIONS

- What important questions do you have for your loved one(s)? Take some time to write these questions down and record your answers. Schedule a date night in which you share your answers.
- If in a relationship, turn to Appendix A and answer the MateMatch questions with your partner.
- What is the difference between feelings of temporary closeness and true intimacy?

2. "Clicking" with Online Dating

Once considered taboo, online dating has become a more commonplace practice amongst contemporary daters. While many people have a more positive view of online dating than they did in the past, others fail to see the benefits. Some still view those who use dating sites as desperate, or they have had negative experiences, such as encountering people who had taken liberties when describing themselves online.[1,2]

Despite the differences in opinion about people who use online dating platforms, there is no doubt that usage is on the rise. One in 10 Americans have used a dating site or mobile app, and 23% have met their spouses or long-term partner through such sites.[1,2] Furthermore, 38% of Americans who are single and actively looking for a partner have used online dating at one point or another and 5% of Americans who are currently married or in a long-term relationship met their partners online.[2]

Online dating may provide a platform for people who are overcommitted in other aspects of life (e.g., work) and have little time to screen hundreds of applicants in person to meet their matches. In fact, these websites provide "increased information about a wider pool of potential partners than usually available in face-to-face encounters"[3] for individuals who are seeking partners.

Researchers note that online dating sites can help a user search for those who share similarities, interests, and values. Users can also search by specific demographics.[4]

Specifically, there are three main services provided by online dating sites:
1. access to potential partners,
2. the ability to communicate, using mediated channels before meeting in person, and
3. the option of being matched using romantic compatibility algorithms.[5]

Some sites, such as OKCupid® and Match.com®, allow the user to look through thousands of profiles, with the option of filtering based on indicated preferences. This enables the user to view and screen potential partners. Other sites, like eHarmony®, use questionnaires to determine the best "match," and send you profiles every few days.

Many sites use an algorithm to create matches and determine compatibility. While most sites keep this information private, OKCupid presents its algorithm on the site. Every time a user answers a question on the site, they collect the following information:
1. "Your answer,
2. How you'd like someone else to answer, and
3. How important the question is to you."[6]

However, OKCupid notes that there is always a margin of error and, "Even though two users have satisfied each other on a few common questions, they may not *actually* be a good match. That is, while the set of questions you've both answered...is small, we can't have much confidence in the match percentage yielded by the...calculations."[6] The site always provides the user with the lowest possible percentage a match can be. Thus, they are conservative in their match identification. The more questions a user answers, the more confident he/she can be in the match percentage presented.[6] Ultimately, although the format of the sites may differ, the goal is still the same: to help users form a romantic connection with another person.

So what do I think about these sites? Despite the chance that the person you are talking to is misrepresenting him/herself and some peoples' resistance to use this form of dating, I am 100% confident that these sites are more than capable of doing what they advertise. Why? Because online dating worked for me. Without one of these sites, I wouldn't have crossed paths with my husband.

Friends who consider me an online dating success story often ask which site works the best. While some, such as those that provide a vast array of profiles rather than sending users matches, are more time consuming and a little daunting, I don't think any one site is better than the others. The only surefire way to come across that lasting connection is when the person you are meant to spend the rest of your life with happens to be on the same site at the exact same time that you're there. Not only that, but you also both need to be at the point in the process where you are not seriously dating anyone else and are ready to jump in to a new relationship with both feet. At that point, all you need is one little click.

TAKE HOME TIPS/QUESTIONS

- **If looking for a partner, take some time to explore the online dating options that exist. Decide if you are interested in a profile-based site, such as Match.com® or a site more tailored to matching people, such as eHarmony®.**
- **Talk to some of your friends about their online success stories.**

III. It's Not You, It's Me: The Art and Science of Mate Choice

1. Finding Your Needle in the Haystack

When people approach searching for their ideal mate, they often have a list of non-negotiables. While it is important to make sure that your partner meets certain criteria, it is vital to realize that the more boxes we require someone to "check off," the narrower we make our dating pool. In doing so, we may overlook a potentially wonderful match.

Peter Backus, Professor in the Department of Economics at the University of Warwick in the United Kingdom, brilliantly applied the Drake Equation to examine just how many women were in his dating pool.[1] The Drake Equation[2] is a series of estimations used to generate a final educated guess, initially purposed to determine the number of civilizations capable of supporting extraterrestrial life in our galaxy. In using this equation, Backus put in all the parameters he used when searching for a partner to come up with an estimation of the number of women out there for him.

Though I am now happily married, I will illustrate this

by employing the search criteria I used several ̶, when online dating. All data comes from the 2015 census. Based upon information provided by the U.S. Census Bureau,[3] New York City has 8,550,405 people. Of these inhabitants, 47.5% are male, which equates to a total of 4,061,442 men.

- Of that number, 33.3% are between the ages of 25 and 44, bringing me to 1,352,460 potential mates.
- Education is important to me, and being that 35.5% of people have a bachelor's degree or higher, I now have the option of 480,123 men.
- As I am of the Jewish faith, and have a preference for a Jewish partner, this takes me down to 43,691 potential partners, since 9.1% of the population in New York City is Jewish.
- Forty-four percent of the population is unattached, and since I want my partner to be exclusive, so there is no one else in the way of our potential union, this takes me to 19,224 matches.
- I'm 5'9", and I tend to feel uneasy when I am much taller than my date, so being that 75% of men are taller than 5'8", I am now down to 14,418 matches.

In Backus' paper, he notes that he is likely to find 5% of women attractive, and 5% of women would find him attractive. However, Hannah Fry, mathematician and author of *The Mathematics of Love*[4] notes that this number is much too conservative. Instead, she opts for using 20%. Therefore, if I am likely to find 20% of these men attractive (2,883 matches), 20% of these men find me attractive (576 matches), and 20% are likely to match me in terms of personality...

This means that, out of the 8,550,405 people in New York City, I have 115 potential matches.

I present this calculation, not to scare you, but to

indicate to you just how special and rare the person you are with, or will be with, actually is. Keep in mind that the more parameters that you put in to the equation, the narrower your potential pool.

I now leave you to your calculations and your search for that special someone.

TAKE HOME TIPS/QUESTIONS
- **What are your non-negotiables? Take some time to list them. Review the list to determine if the items are all non-negotiable or if there is some wiggle room.**
- **Use the Drake Equation and your list of non-negotiables to examine how many people are in your dating pool. Add in and remove the items that have more wiggle room so you can see how these alter the size of your dating pool.**

2. More Choices, More Problems

Psychologist Barry Schwartz coined the term "paradox of choice,"[1] which posits that as we are afforded more choices, the increase in options can lead to higher levels of anxiety. For example, if you are in a town with only one restaurant, you know that you will get good food at that restaurant, most likely run into some friends while dining out, and have an all-around good time. Now, picture yourself on Restaurant Row in Manhattan, with an overwhelming amount of options. It is much more challenging to pick a place and definitively know that you are getting the best food. Therefore, too many choices can lead to problems.

When presented with multiple options, such as the hundreds to thousands of profiles you may find on popular dating or swipe-based matching sites, it is seldom the case that one is clearly the better choice. If one profile was clearly superior, the other options wouldn't even be under consideration. What is more realistic is that, when given the choice (for instance between two colleges, career paths, or mates), you have to weigh the pros and cons, and there are often doubts.

Doubt leads to dissonance, and the more important the decision, the greater that dissonance can be. As I tell my psychology students, there are two simple ways to resolve this dissonance (or uneasiness)- change your belief, or change your behavior. If you apply such resolution to dating, you can either justify that the person you are with is in fact the best option for you, even if you are not sure, OR choose to date someone else. Bouncing back and forth between alternatives is colloquially termed "yo-yo dating." In the case of yo-yo dating,[2] people are just flip-flopping between alternatives to reduce the tension experienced as a result of doubting their mate choice.

The influence of the media is another major issue that may lead to this search for other alternatives. We are constantly being bombarded with movies portraying main characters who end up finding true love. This is not reality- not everyone is going to have someone who shows up in a horse-drawn carriage, with a dozen long-stemmed roses as he/she gets down on one knee and proposes marriage. This unrealistic view of love may lead us on a constant search for the next best thing, and when we fail to find it, to go back to what was comfortable and familiar.

Rather than spending all of your time thinking about whether or not you can do better, it is important to be present in your relationship. Think about the person that you are currently with, and if you are able to say with confidence that you are feeling loved, cared for, and fulfilled, then you should value what you have. If your answer is no, then it is important to find a better relationship and not to turn back.

A great sign of a healthy relationship is a situation in which both individuals give all they have, without expecting anything in return. Rather, each person is devoting him/herself to the relationship and the other person for the sheer joy of it. Renowned researcher John Gottman says that a very big problem in relationships is when people keep track of what each member puts into and takes out of their "emotional bank account," essentially adopting a tit-for-tat philosophy.

When both partners genuinely care for one another, they give without expecting anything and both turn inward and invest into that bank account.[3] In my opinion, getting something back is just the icing on the cake.

TAKE HOME TIPS/QUESTIONS

- **Are you questioning your current relationship? If so, create a list of benefits and drawbacks associated with your partnership. Determine if the benefits derived are enough to outweigh the drawbacks experienced.**
- **Are you in an on-again off-again/yo-yo relationship? If so, take some time to think about why you keep leaving your partner to explore other options and what keeps you coming back.**

IV. It's Something in the Way He/She Looks: Features and Physical Attraction

1. Features that Signal Attractiveness: The Kylie Jenner Effect

After the youngest Kardashian sister admitted that she has benefitted from temporary lip fillers, the internet began buzzing with **#KylieJennerChallenge**, as people all over the world put their lips to bottles and sucked in to create a fuller, plumper lip. Why is it that girls are interested in obtaining Kylie's plump pout? Is it some sort of obsession with looking like a Kardashian, or is there more to it? Although the answer may be a little bit of both, there is indeed a psychological component to the desire to obtain these features.

Facial features serve as a cue of attractiveness. A great deal of research on facial attractiveness tends to focus on symmetry, in which both sides of the face are proportional and perfectly mirror one another. Based on principles of evolutionary psychology, there are three major cues that underpin our "...biologically significant assessments of mate value: symmetry, averageness, and nonaverage sexually dimorphic features."[1] The latter are physical traits which differ between the sexes (such as reproductive organs). With regard to these features, men tend to prefer women with large eyes, small noses, small chins, narrow cheeks, high eyebrows, and large, full-lipped smiles. Other research makes note that large lips on women suggest a strong mating potential.[2]

Another facial feature linked to mate value, which is highlighted on Kylie Jenner's face, is eyes. Women often choose to use eye liner or mascara to frame and exaggerate the size of their eyes. Large eyes are considered a baby-like or neotenous feature. Nobel Prize winning ethologist Konrad Lorenz introduced the idea that the physical features of infants will activate the innate desire in adults to take care of them.

Other researchers[3] note that these characteristics, which imply "babyness," differentiate infants from adults, and include such features as a large head relative to the body, large forehead and eyes, as well as protruding cheeks. Research has shown that adults show a preference for, and make more positive evaluations of infant faces when compared to adult faces, with these positive evaluations of infants most pronounced amongst females. Still other work[4] has shown that younger appearing adults are also more attractive than more mature appearing adults. In fact, younger individuals may be preferred because the baby-like features elicit positive caretaking responses from others.[5]

These standards of beauty appear to be largely universal; and being that people of all cultures exhibit the same preferences, it suggests that there is an evolutionary basis to attraction. Another celebrity who appears to have won the evolutionary jackpot: Angelina Jolie, with her large curved forehead, big eyes, and pronounced lips. So when someone shares the age old adage *beauty is in the eyes of the beholder*, you can respond, "No, it is in the face of the subject."

TAKE HOME TIPS/QUESTIONS

- Examine pictures of celebrities and notice which features they highlight and how they accentuate them. What might these celebrities be doing to increase the salience of their neotenous features?
- Examine how you/your significant other/friends apply makeup. How might you/they be highlighting neotenous features?

2. From Bratz® to Natural Beauties

In the previous chapter, I wrote about how both men and women prefer those who display neotenous (e.g., baby-like) features over adult features and rate those who exhibit them as more attractive.[1] So what happens when toymakers manipulate these baby-like features to give off a sexualized vibe? Enter, the Bratz dolls.

Bratz, owned by MGA Entertainment, is a line of dolls that is very popular with today's children. Bratz have seen a great deal of controversy in their time on the market, as they are often scantily clad and heavily made up.

The American Psychological Association (APA) formed the Task Force on the Sexualization of Girls in response to public concern over the growing problem of sexualization of children and adolescent females. Researchers have found that it is often females upon which sexuality is imposed, especially in the media.[2,3] Not surprisingly, the task force has made mention of the Bratz dolls, noting their "sexualized clothing such as miniskirts, fishnet stockings, and feather boas." This task force stated

in its annual report[2] that there are negative consequences for both girls, and society as a whole, as a result of the sexualization of females. They differentiate sexualization from healthy sexuality, which focuses on an understanding of the body and having the knowledge to express sexuality in a way that enriches one's life.[4] Sexualization involves any of the following four components:
1. a person's value comes from his/her sexual appearance or behavior;
2. the person is objectified;
3. physical attractiveness is associated with being sexy; and/or
4. sexuality is imposed upon the person.[2]

The APA summary notes that presenting females in a highly sexualized manner likely affects both females and males. Girls may engage in self-objectification,[3,5] whereby they treat their own bodies as the subjects of others' desires. Males may start to objectify and harass girls in order to make girls conform to the hypersexualized ideal portrayed in the media. This harassment will likely continue even after the girls have conformed to this standard, as it does not portray girls as people to be valued. Studies show that sexualization can negatively impact females in terms of their cognitive, physical, and mental functioning, as well as their sexuality, attitudes, and beliefs. The task force notes that although most studies have focused on adolescents and adults, these findings likely generalize to younger populations.[2]

Science communicator and artist Sonia Singh may have one approach to combating this problem. After purchasing several Bratz dolls from flea markets and local shops, she set out to give them a "make under" to restore their natural beauty. She created Tree Change Dolls®,[6] natural looking dolls which mirror the girls who play with them. In a matter of weeks, her videos went viral and she now has a huge social media following.

Her husband notes that many dolls, such as Bratz, alter

their appearance for the benefit of other people, "...whereas Sonia's dolls are doing it for themselves."[7] To follow the dolls' transformations and to get inspiration to create your own, see the Tree Change Dolls website: http://treechangedolls.tumblr.com. Perhaps with people like Sonia presenting more realistic versions of girls, we are moving a step in the right direction.

TAKE HOME TIPS/QUESTIONS

- **Go to the toy store and examine popular dolls such as Bratz® and Barbie®. What similarities/differences do they have from the toys you played with as a child? How might the features affect how we feel about the toys? What messages might these toys convey based on the way that they are designed?**

V. War of the Sexes: Gender Differences in Dating and Relationships

1. Do Women Have to Downplay Their Intelligence to Secure a Date?

An interesting study was published in November 2015,[1] which demonstrated that when evaluating "psychologically distant targets" (e.g., more abstract individuals/ hypothetical romantic partners), men prefer women who are more intelligent. However, when rating "psychologically near targets," (e.g., specific potential mates), men were less attracted to women who outperformed them. Essentially what this suggests is that men hypothetically want a smart partner, but when faced with the possibility of meeting an intelligent woman, their superior skills scare them off. Many of my successful friends have been saying this for years, lamenting the fact that men don't want to date smart women. They have felt the need to downplay their successes or jobs to secure the highly coveted second date. So is this true? Do intelligent women have to fear revealing their accomplishments to potential partners?

When selecting a mate, we consider several key factors, such as similarity, attractiveness, and potential to elicit an increased level of physiological arousal. With regard to similarity, it is the idea that "birds of a feather, flock together," rather than "opposites attract" that holds true. Buston and Emlen (2003) discussed the likes-attract hypothesis,[2] in which individuals' self-perception on one trait is related to mate preference of that same trait. Therefore, an intelligent individual should be more likely to choose an intelligent mate.

A colleague and I[3] recently examined the idea of the likes-attract hypothesis with a focus on academic motivation to explore education related mate preferences. It was hypothesized that participants who rated themselves as more intrinsically motivated to succeed in school would value factors relating to education and ambition when considering a potential mate. We examined 374 participants and found that as intrinsic motivation increased, the importance of education and intelligence in a mate also increased. Also, as motivation increased, being a college graduate was rated as more desirable for a potential mate. However, it is important to realize that participants were rating hypothetical traits, which are abstract. As we didn't explore actual mate selection behaviors experimentally, how these beliefs would translate into actual real-life mate selection is still unclear.

Tesser's self-evaluation maintenance model[4] states that we base our self-evaluation off of close relationships. Therefore, the success of someone close (e.g., a significant other) may make us feel threatened. If a partner is very intelligent and successful, and these are attributes that are relevant to our own self-definition, our self-evaluation is lowered. Based on this, the person who feels threatened would need to leave the relationship. Preventing this comparison would maintain his/her positive self-evaluation.

Research has shown that males report lower self-esteem when their girlfriends score high on tests[5] (and the effect isn't always something that they are conscious of). Women don't seem to be affected in this same way. Women are more likely to experience what is known as "reflected glory," in that they share in the success of others, and as such, would show a boost in self-esteem when their male partner does well or succeeds. This may be in part because women are more likely to view themselves as part of the relationship, and therefore feel a sense of accomplishment when one member succeeds, compared to men who use the success of the other as a standard by which to compare themselves.

Attachment styles may also come into play here. Those who have a secure attachment to their mate, will be more satisfied with and confident in their relationships, as securely attached people have positive expectations about relationship partners.[6] A securely attached man wouldn't worry about a woman stealing the spotlight, but instead would allow her to seek her own personal success, support her along the way, and value her accomplishments.

The dating game has changed quite a bit from previous generations, in that now women are pursuing higher degrees and careers, which makes them much more selective when it comes to choosing their mates. Also, with easier access to the dating pool (e.g., online dating, social media, etc.), people are given more options, and essentially are able to "customize" their partners (by selecting their preferences).

As with any cultural shift, it will take a while before the environmental conditions begin to impact behavior. Some research suggests that men want a successful woman in theory, but do not actually select this woman in practice. Eventually, the pressure put forth to select someone that can successfully navigate a challenging world will influence the choices people make in selecting their mates.

TAKE HOME TIPS/QUESTIONS

- Think about the advice your friends have given you/you have given your friends when it comes to first date conversations. Are there any topics that people have told you to steer clear of, or any information to intentionally leave out? Why might this be?
- Being that many women feel the need to downplay their intelligence, what implications does this have for society as a whole? What do you think this means in terms of how women are viewed/treated compared to men?

2. First Date Interactions: Does Gender Play a Role?

Researchers have noted that women are more selective when it comes to choosing their dating partners.[1] Therefore, it is important that the interaction on the first date is positive and a connection is made.

In studying the conversations between men and women, researchers have found that a good connection is created when the conversation is aligned toward women and away from men, with women engaged in the encounter.[2] However, other research has suggested that men are expected to play the dominant role in a conversation, with women merely acting as supporting characters.[2] As there are conflicting reports, this area still warrants investigation. The interaction scenario which leads to the best outcome based on first impressions is important to study, as this could potentially help guide daters in the right direction.

Non-verbal behavior is another area in which gender differences have been highlighted. Karl Grammer (1989) states that, as females have an overall higher investment in a relationship, they also have a greater risk. Being that this is the case, they tend to be more indirect and "...employ non-committal non-verbal invitation, in this way exerting control."[3] Males, then, are left to interpret their messages.

There is evidence which suggests that gender stereotypes are still prevalent in modern dating encounters.[4] As a result, when it comes to the beginning of potential new relationships, specifically the events of the first date, more research is needed.

A study conducted through the Self-Awareness and Bonding Lab (SABL)[5] examined differences between males and females on first dates. All participants took a researcher-designed survey which consisted of demographic questions, as well as 30 statements detailing potential behaviors of a romantic partner on a first date. An example of such a behavior was, "He/she hugs you when he/she meets you." Participants were told to rate each behavior on a 5-point Likert scale to elicit their perception of how attracted their potential partners were to them. All answers were confidential. Rather than provide you with the specific statistics, those which were found to be significant will be highlighted below, along with take-home tips.

DISCLAIMER: The take-home tips reflect the data found as a result of this specific study, and do not reflect my personal beliefs. I would like you to be informed by the research. In addition, as a majority of the sample was heterosexual, the data are presented in terms of a date involving a male/female dyad.

Below is the list of behaviors that **FEMALES view as signaling attraction** on the part of their dates. Therefore, if a male displays the following behaviors, a female will view them as a positive indication of the date's physical attraction to her.

1. Date maintains a lively conversation
    Take home (for partner): Maintain the flow of the conversation (Have a plan A, B, and C)
2. Date spoke mostly about the participant (in this case, the female)
    Take home (for partner): Women like when the conversation is centered on them
3. Date discusses future plans
    Take home (for partner): Show that you are thinking far beyond tonight
4. Date makes positive comments about your physical appearance
    Take home (for partner): Compliments can go a long way
5. Date focuses on similarities
    Take home (for partner): Try to relate to her on some level and focus on what you have in common
6. Date offers to pay
    Take home (for partner): Be chivalrous, offer to pay
7. Date suggests extending the evening
    Take home (for partner): Don't be too quick to get out of there. Don't plan a second date that evening with another woman!
8. Date attempts to hug or kiss you at the end of the evening
    Take home (for partner): Women infer your feelings for them based on attempts for physical contact
9. Date calls a few hours later to schedule another date
    Take home (for partner): If you like her, let her know...and quickly!

The following are what **MALES view as signaling attraction** on the part of their dates. Therefore, if a female displays the following behaviors, the male will view her as signaling that she is attracted to him.

1. Date talks about herself
    Take home (for partner): Go ahead women, share! **MATCH**
2. Date diverts the conversation to sex
    Take home (for partner): Don't be afraid to let your guard down
3. Date attempts to split the cost of the meal
    Take home (for partner): This isn't 1950, offer to pay! **MISMATCH**
4. Date doesn't initiate contact, but responds right away
    Take home (for partner): Don't make the first move, but be responsive. (Personally, I take issue with this).

You will notice from the first set of results, that both men and women view it as a positive indication of attraction when the woman talks about herself. However, there is a clear mismatch when it comes to paying for the meal. Women want men to offer (as it signals that they are attracted to the women), whereas men want women to offer to split the cost of the meal.

Below are the behaviors that **FEMALES view as signaling LESS attraction** on the part of the males during the first date.

1. Date shakes hand upon meeting
    Take home (for partner): Go in for the hug
2. Date focuses on differences between you two

during conversation
> **Take home (for partner):** Don't highlight your differences, focus on similarities

3. Date discusses past relationships
   > **Take home (for partner):** Don't bring up the past
4. Date waves goodbye at the end of the date
   > **Take home (for partner):** Again, go in for the hug
5. Date doesn't initiate contact, and upon your initiation, responds a few days later
   > **Take home (for partner):** If she contacts you, respond to her right away!
6. Date doesn't initiate contact, and upon your initiation doesn't respond to you
   > **Take home (for partner):** If you like her, don't ghost her

Finally, below are the behaviors that **MALES view as signaling LESS attraction** on the part of the females.

1. NOTHING!
   > **Take home (for partner):** They will always think you like them!

Based on the findings it appears as if women, to a larger extent than men, use behaviors as cues of their dates' attraction to them. This makes sense as previous research has shown that women tend to be the pickier sex.[2] The results suggest that females are much more selective and potentially judgmental about behaviors when on a first date. Males didn't allow any behaviors to serve as a signal that their date was less attracted to them, whereas females read into many of their date's behaviors as a negative indication of their feelings. This is important, because, with a better understanding of what our actions signal to others, we can tailor our behaviors to influence the type of first impression we make.

TAKE HOME TIPS/QUESTIONS

- **What "deal breakers" have there been for you on previous first dates? Why might these have been "deal breakers"? Think about why each "deal breaker" presented an issue for you. Knowing these will help you understand a little more about yourself and what you are looking for in a partner.**

VI. Actions are Worth More than Words: Expressing Love for Your Partner

1. Giving the Gift of an Experience this Valentine's Day

As Valentine's Day approaches, people experience stress and often spend countless hours searching for the "perfect gift." Many people look forward to showing their partners how much they are loved by exchanging gifts, while others are filled with anxiety in trying to pick out the best item. You can hardly walk down the street without being bombarded by store windows featuring giant people-sized teddy bears and equally large heart shaped boxes of chocolate. For those in relationships, picking out the perfect present is of utmost importance, as the gift ideally symbolizes our love for the other person. This is because "gift-giving involves both the objective value of a gift and the symbolic meaning of the exchange."[1] Before making your final decision between jewelry or something practical like a pair of winter gloves, consider giving your partner an experience.

While picking a tangible item may seem like the standard approach, we can often go wrong with material gifts, as we may select an item in the wrong size, color, or style.[2] This can be upsetting to both the gifter and the receiver. This scenario demonstrates that the gifter may not know important information about the receiver such as color preference or size, and puts the receiver in the position of having to pretend that the item is perfect or run the risk of exchanging it without his/her partner finding out. Having to buy a material item can also be problematic when shopping for the person who seems to have everything. You don't want to buy the person something he/she already owns, and would feel badly selecting something that he/she doesn't actually want.

Purchasing an experience, such as a day at the spa, a cooking class, tour, or bike riding adventure may solve any concerns you have when it comes to focusing on the "right" material gift. As an added bonus, research reveals that experiences make people happier than material items.[3] Qualitative research which set out to examine the gift-giving experience through 52 in-depth interviews demonstrated that gift receivers not only value the gift given, but also experience gratitude for the thought that went into making the selection.[2] First, selecting an experience that the receiver will enjoy shows a great deal of thought and effort. This leads to more appreciation from the receiver than when choosing a gift randomly off of a wish list. The selection of experiences enables the gift giver to be creative and demonstrate more intimate knowledge of the receiver. Also, rather than having to pick out a specific item, you can base your choice of gift on knowledge of the recipients' passions and his/her likes and dislikes.[2] More creativity and effort can also be embedded into presenting the experience gift, as intangibility allows for a clever presentation and revelation.

Second, focusing on giving an experience addresses the problem of what to get a person who appears to have everything. Even if a person has already taken a cooking class, perhaps they have not had this same experience with you, thereby altering the event in a meaningful way. These gifts are recalled positively, as both the giver and the receiver are able to create new, happy memories.[2] Finally, quality time is embedded in experience gift-giving, as the present itself opens up the possibility of sharing the experience. Many gift givers recalled during the interview that the receivers, when presented with an experience, chose to take the gifter along, creating a joint experience. This can enhance the quality of your relationships as "sharing is deemed important by both donors and recipients as it is used to expand personal horizons and to nurture relationships."[2]

So now that you know that people would rather receive experience gifts and that experiences demonstrate a more intimate level of knowledge about the receiver, where might you look for such gifts? Below is a list of websites that allow you to search by location and type of experience to perfectly tailor the gift for your loved one:

- **http://www.cloud9living.com/** Search by type of experience and location to select an interesting event
- **https://coursehorse.com/** Select courses on a variety of topics in LA, NY, Chicago, or online.
- **https://www.livingsocial.com** While this site has material gifts, it also offers discounts on events in all major cities.

Good luck gift shopping and enjoy your new experiences!

TAKE HOME TIPS/QUESTIONS
- **Visit the sites I listed above and look for some potential presents that you can give to your friends and loved ones.**
- **Give yourself the gift of an experience!**

2. Playing Hard to Get Potentially Fried this Frog

Let's recap: Ben and Jen, Blake and Miranda, Gavin and Gwen, Taylor and Calvin, Taylor and Tom, Brad and Angelina, and finally Miss Piggy and Kermit. There was a wave of celebrities announcing their decisions to end their relationships between the last few weeks of 2015 and now. Being that Miss Piggy's announcement hit me particularly hard, I decided to analyze just what went wrong. Was it her frequent temper tantrums and karate kicks? Her obsession with fame? Lack of a social support network due to their interspecies relationship? Or perhaps it was the way she approached her relationship with Kermit from the beginning?

Miss Piggy was very clear and direct in her declaration of love for Kermit. In recalling how they met, she said "The first time I saw Kermit, Moi's future flashed before me in a pink, rosy glow. The first time Kermit saw Moi, he was lost for words."[1] She was clear about her love for Kermit from the outset, but were her advances too strong? In a series of studies conducted in the 1970s, researchers[2] examined whether playing hard to get makes a woman more or less attractive. They began by asking college-aged men why they preferred the elusive, "hard to get" woman. Common responses were:

- If she is choosy, she must be popular
- She is more valuable
- We enjoy the challenge
- She is more desirable[2]

These college-aged students may have been on to something, as a number of psychological theories provide support for the idea that the hard to get woman should be more appealing. For example, dissonance theory puts forth the argument that the more energy expended toward a goal, the more appreciative the person who pursued the goal will be once it is attained. If Kermit had to work to win Miss Piggy's affection, he would have valued the effort he put in, and in turn valued her. Further, based on learning theory, frustration may increase a person's drive and the impact of the reward provided. A person that is a little standoffish could frustrate a potential suitor, thereby heightening his drive level. This would make the acceptance of his advances a larger reward. Also, based on this theory, elusiveness may be associated with value, as there is more competition for desirable partners.[2] If Miss Piggy wasn't so forthcoming with her attraction for Kermit, she would have maximized the impact of her desire for him.

So did she play it all wrong? Was she simply too intense during the course of their relationship? In the research mentioned above, the researchers demonstrated that in fact there are two components that determine how much a man will like a woman. The first component is how hard or easy she is for him to get and the second is how hard or easy she is for other men to obtain. If a woman is too easy to get, her affection is not seen as anything special. However, if she is perceived as too hard to get, men run the risk of rejection. She may also be seen as rigid or cold.[2]

Thus, the perfect combination is a woman who is perceived as hard to get for everyone else, but not so hard for the one doing the pursuing (e.g. Kermit). For example, in one of their studies, Walster and colleagues manipulated how hard or easy five fictitious women were to get, and examined the responses of 71 college students. The subjects were told that they were going to be matched up with the women, and that three of them already had the opportunity to examine their male matches (with the subjects' profiles included). A woman appeared easy to get when she indicated that she was enthusiastic about dating all five men assigned to her. She appeared hard to get when she was not willing to date any of the men assigned to her. Finally, she appeared to be selective when she was easy for the subject to get (she rated him high), but hard for everyone else to get (rated them low). Nearly all subjects preferred to date the selective woman. Specifically, they found that "[i]f a woman has a reputation for being hard to get, but for some reason she is easy for the subject to get, she should be maximally appealing."[2]

Now Miss Piggy seemed to brush all others off, and made it clear to Kermit that he was the one for her. This would make her selective, so what exactly is the problem? It is important to realize that this study viewed the process only from the male perspective, and didn't take into account how women view men during mate selection. Perhaps the demise of their relationship had nothing to do with Miss Piggy, but was a result of Kermit's actions. It may be the case that their relationship ended because Kermit didn't properly value Miss Piggy. She may have gotten tired of *him* having played too hard to get for too long. The exchange below illustrates his indifference to her perfectly:

> **Miss Piggy:** Kermit, do you notice that every time we have a beautiful girl on the show, you forget about me?
> **Kermit:** Uh, yeah, well, we could have a

seal act on the show, and I might forget about you.[3]

Good luck with the seals Kermit, you just lost your pig.

**During the Muppets TV show finale, Miss Piggy, under the influence of liquid courage, professed her love for Kermit. This resonated with him and it appeared as if he was going to try and make things work. I'm wishing these two the very best.

TAKE HOME TIPS/QUESTIONS

- **Have you ever played hard to get with someone? Why? What message do you think this sent to the other person and how might this have affected your relationship?**

VII. Understanding our Bodies: The Role of Physiological Arousal and Emotions

1. Misattribution in Paradise

Somehow, even with my reality TV addiction, I was able to avoid *The Bachelor* for the past 20+ seasons, *Bachelor Pad*, and *Bachelor in Paradise*. However, during the summer of 2015, at the request of a friend, I sat down to watch the second season of *Bachelor in Paradise*. I was immediately sucked in. A revolving door of men and women moved into a villa in Vallarta-Nayarit, Mexico, all with the hopes of finding love. Each week a few cast members would be given date cards by the host of the show, instructing them to pick partners to accompany them on various excursions. While some of the date cards cast members were given led to private dinners and fantasy suites (think rose petals, champagne, and private hotel rooms), a large number of the dates involved more active plans, such as wrestling matches, bungee jumping, dancing at a club, and jet skiing. People seemed to be really into each other on the dates, but would often question their feelings shortly after, when back on the serene beach. Was the post-date letdown because there were so many good looking unattached people around to pull their attention away from the partner they just went on a date with? Or was it something more—perhaps something physiological?

The famous Dutton and Aron (1974)[1] bridge study tested the idea of misattribution of arousal, in which the arousal experienced in a particular setting (e.g., while on a shaky bridge) is mislabeled and associated with something else.[2] In this particular study, men crossed either a high shaky bridge or a low-to-the-ground bridge and were approached by a female research assistant. In both instances, she showed them an ambiguous picture and told them to describe what was happening. She also gave them her number and instructed them to call her should they have any questions about the experiment. Those who crossed the high bridge were much more likely to call the female and incorporate sexual imagery in with their descriptions of the pictures they saw. This is because the men who were on the higher bridge associated the physiological arousal they felt (e.g., racing heart, sweaty palms, etc.) with feelings of attraction for the woman.

Other studies have replicated the arousal-attraction link finding that couples want to be closer to each other after watching a high arousal movie, compared to a low arousal movie.[3] In another study, participants were approached as they were waiting on the line for a roller coaster ride or after they had just gotten off. They were asked to rate the attractiveness of an average, opposite gendered picture of a person as well as the person they were planning to sit with, both before and after the ride. Results demonstrated that for those who weren't with a romantic partner, attractiveness ratings for both the seatmate and picture increased after they had gotten off the ride.[4]

Returning to the *Bachelor in Paradise*, the show began with Ashley I. and Jared riding ATVs through the jungle and forming a connection with one another. By the end of the season, however, Jared didn't feel a connection with Ashley I. and opted to leave paradise without giving her a rose during one of the final ceremonies. This rejection occurred despite her pouring her heart out to him and multiple attempts to prove that they were meant for one another. But the initial connection they felt to one another may never have happened without the potential effects of misattribution of arousal. Once the thrill of riding ATVs wore off, it was splitsville. One can only hope that the relationship formed between Tanner and Jade, the couple who left Mexico engaged, was real rather than the result of the increased arousal experienced in paradise. If not, I suggest they go on a lot of roller coaster rides in the near future to keep the momentum going.

TAKE HOME TIPS/QUESTIONS
- **Identify date activities that can increase your physiological arousal, such as going on a hike.**
- **Think about and record examples of times when you have relied on cues from your body to interpret a situation you were faced with (e.g. realizing how scary walking alone at night may be after noticing your racing heart).**

2. Why Do We Watch Romantic Movies During Winter Storms?

While the winter of 2016 was relatively mild for those of us in the Northeast, we were hit with Jonas, a very severe storm resulting in more than 36" of snow in some places, late in the season. While some of us braved the weather to walk our dogs, dig out our cars, or make an emergency trip to the store to pick up the milk we forgot to buy in the days leading up to the storm, the rest of us probably stayed warm indoors and watched TV. After texting my friends to discuss their snowpocalypse plans, I found out that many, like me, were watching romantic movies. Was this all just a pre-Valentine's Day coincidence? The answer lies in research on embodied cognition.

Embodied cognition is a theory which states that perception affects our thinking,[1] people's social experience is not independent of physical and somatic perception,[2] and in fact is "...grounded in physical context and perceptual processes."[3] For example, research has shown that touching warm objects influences peoples' assessments of others; as participants who held a cup of hot coffee rated a random person as warmer and friendlier compared to those who held a cup of cold coffee.[2] The converse is also true, in that emotional experiences can influence physical sensations. In two experiments, researchers found that people literally felt cold or preferred warm food when they experienced being socially excluded, demonstrating that feelings of isolation led people to seek warmth.[2]

A recent research study set out to determine if physical coldness activates the motivation for psychological warmth, which may manifest itself in the preference for romantic movies.[3] Through a series of studies, Hong and Sun supported their hypothesis. In the first study, 53 participants were randomly assigned to either drink hot or cold tea and were presented with information on three movies from each of the following four genres: romance, action, comedy, and thriller. They were then asked to rate how good they thought each movie would be. Participants in the cold drink condition showed a greater preference for romance movies than those in the hot drink condition. However, the ratings for the other genres were not significantly different, demonstrating that the cold only influenced perception of romance movies, not movies in general. Overall, the researchers demonstrated that physical coldness led to increased liking for, or in other words, an increased desire to watch romance movies.[3]

In the second study, the extent to which people associate romance movies with psychological warmth was measured. One hundred forty participants were told to indicate how movies make them feel on a 7-point scale (1 = gives me a cold feeling to 7 = gives me a warm feeling). They were also exposed to the same conditions and asked to rate the movies, as they had in the previous experiment. Results showed that the more participants associated romance movies with psychological warmth, the more they liked these movies. Taken together, these studies show that a physical experience may influence cognitive judgement.[3]

Each winter, as you prepare to endure what may be the coldest and worst part of the year, take a tip from the research and queue up your Netflix for plenty of romance rentals. Not only will they be entertaining, but they may bring you some much needed warmth.

TAKE HOME TIPS/QUESTIONS

- **Think about what foods you tend to gravitate toward when you feel different emotions. Why might you reach for certain foods?**
- **What is your favorite comfort food? Does temperature come into play?**

VIII. The Design of Love: Relationship Structure and Configurations

1. Is Marriage Really Synonymous with Monogamy?

After her husband of 18 years revealed that he had gotten a vasectomy, successful magazine journalist Robin Rinaldi came to the sinking realization that she would not have the family she had once hoped for. Being that she couldn't create the home life she dreamed of, she decided to go down a different path and explore her sexuality. In her book, *The Wild Oats Project*,[1] Rinaldi discusses her quest for passion after she proposed an arrangement in which she would live on her own and be free to take on lovers during the week, while returning home to her role as a wife on the weekends. The book discusses her sexual quest to feel fulfilled as she takes on both male and female lovers and attend workshops geared towards getting in touch with her sexual self. Lest I spoil the end of her intriguing narrative, it would be better to leave you questioning whether or not her marriage was able to sustain the shake-up caused by this mutually, albeit somewhat coerced, agreement. Also, whether or not her marriage survived, it begs the question: Is marriage really synonymous with monogamy?

Relationship Configurations

Although it may be simple to think of a relationship as either monogamous or not, many variations exist, often with fuzzy boundaries. Some researchers[2] use the term *consensually non-monogamous* (CNM) to define any arrangement in which partners have extra-dyadic sexual or romantic relationships (e.g., they sleep with other people). Others[3] use the term "open" relationship to imply a non-monogamous sexual agreement which is characterized by rules that define which extra-dyadic sexual activities are permitted. The term "open" may be flawed as it leaves much open to interpretation.

By and large, an open relationship is really an umbrella term that encompasses any non-monogamous relationship[4]. Under "open relationships," one can find different types including:

- **partnered non-monogamy-** a couple that enjoys extra-dyadic sex
- **swinging-** non-monogamy in social settings
- **polyamory-** a situation in which partners have more than one relationship
- **solo polyamory**- non-monogamous individuals who don't want a primary partner
- **polyfidelity-** three or more people who have made a commitment to one another
- **monogamous/non-monogamous partnership**- one member is monogamous

Typically, the defining feature of the overarching open relationship structure is that the two individuals consider each other to be the primary partners in the relationship. Dan Savage, host of the Savage Lovecast notes, "People simply are not always wired to be monogamous creatures," and has coined the term "monogam-ish."[5] He has shared that people tend to negatively view those who are monogam-ish, because we typically only hear about the cases in which this type of relationship has failed. In fact, many people may be in these types of relationship configurations, but are not willing to discuss it for fear that they will be seen as sex-crazed deviants.

For Better or For Worse,[6] a documentary nominated for an Academy Award in 1993, followed couples who have made it over the 50 year marriage mark. Ninety year old, Dan Trupin, says through laughter, "Monogamy is monotony." His wife, Sophie, later explains, over a dinner scene with the family, that it is the job of the woman to look the other way when her man strays, which he inevitably does. Dan Trupin was shocked by his wife's analysis of marriage, and in a later scene, admits to never having loved anyone but her or having been with anyone else during their time together.

However, it was in this same documentary that Howard and Cecil Waite, a couple married for 63 years, discuss the arrangement in which he would drop Cecil off at her boyfriend's house on his way to his girlfriend's house. They would spend hours with their other partners before meeting up at the end of the day. All this, but they never once considered divorce. This couple's scenario, in particular, usually creates the most discomfort amongst my students when they view the documentary in class. They wonder how this couple can have a happy and fulfilled relationship while essentially cheating on one another. But is this really cheating? The answer may not be so simple.

Satisfaction Derived from Relationships

The idea that individuals cannot be satisfied in an open relationship mostly originated from our heterocentric view of monogamy, in which we use heterosexual relationships as our basis for understanding all forms of coupling. More than half of men who have extramarital sex reported that they were happy or very happy in their marriages.[4,7] The two main ingredients needed for an open relationship to work are honesty and boundaries. Non-monogamous couples must disclose all of the information regarding their extra-dyadic pairings, as well as create a clear set of rules before engaging in such relationships. Once accomplished, the couple can enjoy a happy and fulfilling relationship. In fact, research has shown that open relationships allow the members to feel "...like they have created a relationship that reflects their authenticity and self-awareness."[4] The individuals also benefit from a deeper level of honesty about sexual behavior and desires.

Social conventions have reinforced the idea that to be with one partner is moral and the norm. Individuals in open relationships are often portrayed negatively. It is, unfortunately, typical for therapists to associate non-monogamy with relationship dysfunction and individual psychopathology[8] as well as suggest that relationships of this nature indicate that the primary relationship is troubled.[2] However, just because we don't talk about our behaviors out in the open does not mean that they don't exist. Perhaps we would all benefit from a more honest discussion of what goes on behind closed doors after the vows have been taken. With a more accurate look at the nature of relationships, we can potentially mitigate the bias associated with certain configurations.

TAKE HOME TIPS/QUESTIONS

- **Take some time to examine the assumptions you make about a person and his/her relationship satisfaction based upon the type of relationship he/she has. Why might you jump to such conclusions?**
- **Write down the potential pros and cons of different relationship structures (monogamy, polyamory, etc.). Be sure to keep your list balanced- for every pro, you must include a con.**

2. Polyamory: Understanding Relationship Geometry

Relationship Configurations

When relationships are examined by the media and/or empirical research, the focus is often on the traditional monogamous couple (e.g., one male and one female, two males, or two females). These monogamous relationships are depicted as the natural and healthy ideal.[1] Conversely, the media often portrays those in consensually non-monogamous (CNM) relationships as deviants; and therapists also suggest that the existence of CNM relationships mean the *primary* relationship is troubled.[1] Clearly, there is a stigma surrounding non-monogamy, and therefore, non-monogamy is generally not openly discussed. This is problematic, not only because non-monogamous individuals are often stereotyped, but they also suffer from a lack of support within the therapeutic community. Nicole Graham, a psychiatrist, writes,

> "It is apparent that a lack of awareness of and appreciation for non-traditional relationship

> patterns can have deleterious effects, including but not limited to a lack of objectivity, inadvertent criticism and potential pathologization of individuals, damaged therapeutic alliances, resultant treatment non-adherence, and potentially poorer patient outcomes."[2]

This chapter will discuss why it is so important to understand the various types of relationship configurations that exist, specifically polyamory, as well as provide a first-hand account and a deeper understanding of the polyamorous community. First, it is important to recognize that there are a variety of relationship configurations (see previous chapter).

There are many societal and therapeutic benefits of taking a closer look at CNM relationships. Mental health practitioners must be able to recognize the sexual fluidity both within individuals and their relationship arrangements. Marianne Brandon, a clinical psychologist asks,

> "If we as treators cannot accept and contain the monogamy challenge, how can we help our patients to do the same?...And if we choose to criticize our patients' non-monogamous choices can we still optimally assist them in the intimate challenges for which they seek help? Probably not. And our patients need our help now more than ever"[3]

In order to be able to help those who come in with an "unconventional" relationship style, therapists must address their personal biases, and what better way to do that than by learning more about these relationships?

Polyamory

One particular romantic configuration, which is being discussed more openly in the mainstream media is polyamory. Polyamory is "...characterized by simultaneous consensual romantic relationships with multiple partners."[4] Because of the stigma surrounding non-monogamous relationships, the prevalence of CNM relationships is difficult to determine. However, the Polyamory Group Registry has information on 265 poly groups (e.g., webpages, Meetup® groups, and blogs devoted to polyamory) in 195 countries.[5]

Definition/Structure. Polyamory is defined by researchers as the desire to have multiple relationships.[6] It is considered a form of "ethical non-monogamy" as all partners are aware that the relationship is not monogamous and have agreed upon its terms.[7] A major issue in trying to define and describe polyamory is that there are "...almost as many definitions of the word 'polyamory' as there are people using it."[8] While some may consider it a particular relationship form, others view it as a dedication to values regarding a particular approach to intimacy.[7]

Co-authors, and members of the open community, Dossie Easton (a therapist) and Janet W. Hardy (a writer, publisher, and teacher), note that some people lump swinging, group sex, etc. into polyamory, however the most conservative definition only refers to "...long-term committed multi-partner relationships."[8]

There are two basic types of poly relationship structures. Some are hierarchical, in which there tends to be a primary, secondary, tertiary partner, etc. In this structure, people often live with their "primaries," and love, but don't live with their "secondaries," "tertiaries," etc.[8] There are also nonhierarchical poly relationships, and in such a structure, no one gets any preferential treatment, as all partners are equals. These can look more like constellations, and people at the hub are connected to several others.[8] Easton and Hardy also note that members may form very complex structures, and that the roles within the group will continue to develop, grow and change over time.[8]

Rules. Rules, which may be explicitly stated or inferred, are important as they set the boundaries for a relationship. Easton and Hardy note that "in an open sexual community, it is important to deal with each relationship within its own boundaries."[8] These boundaries can get tricky, and often times are learned through trial and error. When setting boundaries through rules, it is important to both learn from mistakes and allow room for exploration.[8]

"Ideal" relationship. Easton and Hardy state that relationships should be written based upon your own script. This is difficult as it requires a lot of effort and honesty.[8] However, once the work is done, it can be very rewarding. When initiating a poly relationship, ideally all parties would agree at the beginning that the relationship would be open. In cases where this does not happen, one person must bring up the topic of the relationship structure to see how his/her partner feels about it; the sooner, the better.

"Ideal" participants. Easton and Hardy have found that open relationships work best when the initial couple takes care of each other before letting others in.[8] This often requires work and great communication. People must also be comfortable setting and defining their boundaries.

Benefits/Drawbacks. While poly relationships allow individuals to express their love for multiple others and create their own romantic destiny, poly individuals may also face harsh criticism. As mentioned before, many therapists view this type of relationship configuration as deviant.[1] Easton and Hardy note that family members and friends may be hostile and unsupportive.[8] They "...know people who have lost jobs, child custody, and more because the wrong people have become aware of their sexual choices."[8]

Views of Love/Marriage. People often equate a monogamous relationship with a loving relationship, as "...the couple relationship and the model of the core family have been shaped by the cultural ideals bound up with romantic love."[7] Easton and Hardy write, "Our monogamy-centrist culture tends to assume that the purpose and ultimate goal of all relationships- and all sex- is lifelong pair bonding, and that any relationship that falls short of that goal has failed."[8] Assumptions that love is finite should be abandoned, as our capacity for both sex and love is greater than we think.[8] People who identify with polyamory may or may not have multiple partners, however they are in a relationship in which love has the potential to grow eternally.[7]

In reality, people are capable of falling in love with more than one person, at no detriment to their relationship(s) with their other partners. This, to an extent is confirmed by research which shows that "...individuals' relationships with one partner tend to operate relatively independently of their relationships with another partner. Thus, having multiple partners in itself does not appear to have a strong positive or negative effect on dyadic relationships."[4]

Conclusion

Polyamory is being discussed more openly in the mainstream media, and as a result the number of groups and support systems available is on the rise. However, more empirical studies are needed, as research on this population is lacking.

Through my extensive review of the literature focused on polyamory, and discussions with poly-individuals, I have learned about the variety of relationship structures that exist, as well as the importance of starting off with clear expectations regarding boundaries. In order to be in a happy and supportive relationship, a great deal of work is required, as well as the ability to communicate honestly with your partner(s).

Preconceived notions regarding the structure of a relationship can be damaging when it results in the stereotyping of individuals who don't conform to this "standard." By learning more about others, we can become more accepting, and perhaps even learn more about ourselves. Because at the end of the day, what is it really all about?

Love.

TAKE HOME TIPS/QUESTIONS

- **What rules are important for you to have in your relationship? Write these down and plan a conversation with your partner about them.**
- **What beliefs did you grow up with regarding love (e.g. we each have one soul mate)? How do you feel about these beliefs today?**

IX. When the Past Influences Our Present and Future: Thinking About Ex-Partners

1. The Ghost of Relationships Past

Transference is "...a tendency in which representational aspects of important and formative relationships (such as with parents and siblings) can be both consciously experienced and/or unconsciously ascribed to other relationships."[1] Specifically, transference refers to the process by which the feelings that you had for someone (such as a parent) become directed to someone else (such as a therapist or psychoanalyst).[2] The phenomenon of transference may be triggered when a new person resembles someone else, physically or in terms of their personality characteristics. Transference also occurs in everyday life.

For example, a few of my friends have displayed transference when dealing with their significant others. One in particular, who had been cheated on in the past, would transfer the feelings she had for her previous romantic partner to her current boyfriend. After finding out that he was going to be stuck late at work, which was quite often, she would secretly check his email and phone messages. Her feelings of mistrust, which were caused by her previous partner, led to trust issues with and resentment toward her current partner. This eventually created a rift between them. If experiences with the past can influence our future, how might this impact our relationships?

Our past relationships, and the feelings we had for a significant other, can transfer to a subsequent relationship, and ultimately have a profound effect on the new romantic relationship. When is such transference, from one relationship to another, most likely to happen? According to the social-cognitive model of transference,[3] our mental representations of significant others are stored in memory and can transfer to a new person. This transference is typically triggered when the new person resembles the significant other.[3]

The assumptions regarding transference in this context are:

- it occurs in daily life, as well as in psychotherapy
- the content that gets transferred depends upon the specific person
- it occurs for all types of significant others
- the feelings and content that get transferred may change over time[3]

In a classic study on the topic, researchers used an *idiographic research method* in which they first had participants generate sentences to describe a significant other (e.g. "My partner is very giving"). Two weeks later, participants were divided into two groups and were presented with a series of sentences describing one or several *new* target persons. In the experimental condition, participants were exposed to one target who resembled the significant other, as he/she was characterized in terms of the sentences previously provided by the participant. This hypothetical individual was constructed in such a way as to subtly resemble the participant's own partner using positive and negative features from the first session.[4] In the control condition, none of the targets resembled the significant other.

In both conditions, after learning about the new target person, the participants completed a series of measures, such as a recognition memory test. This requires the participants to read sentences describing the target and rate their confidence that the statements provide information describing this previously presented individual. They must be able to discriminate between the target, who may have resembled their significant other, and their actual knowledge of their significant other.

Overall, participants evaluated the targets resembling their own significant other more favorably if their impressions of their partner were positive. Targets who represented negative aspects of their partners were not rated as favorably. Additionally, the researchers examined the participants' facial expressions when reading descriptors about the target person. Participants' facial expressions were more pleasant when learning about a target who resembled a positive significant other rather than a negative significant other. These facial expression changes were not shown in the control, demonstrating that they were a result of transference.[3]

The transference process also influenced how participants' viewed *themselves*. After learning about the new person in the experiment, each participant was instructed to describe him/herself. The researchers looked at how much overlap there was between the description of the significant other and the description of the self that was given. The researchers analyzed how much overlap there was and it was found that self-concept changed. The researchers noted that "...in relation to the new person, one becomes the version of self one is with the significant other."[3] This change was greater in the experimental condition in which the target resembled the participants' significant others, which shows that when exposed to someone similar to a previous partner, you become the version of yourself that you were with that person.

Overall, this study shows that "... past experiences with significant others appear to have a broad and profound impact on present relationships, and transference is critical in this process as it occurs in everyday social relations."[3] Now you may wonder what implications this research has for us in our day-to-day lives. Armed with this information, it is important to reflect on how each relationship has impacted you, and in turn changed how you view yourself. It is also imperative to be cognizant that when someone reminds you of an ex-romantic partner, try not to let the past influence your present. On that same note, being overly optimistic about a new partner, based on past positive associations with an ex, may also be detrimental, as you may not accurately be judging the new relationship objectively. What this work really shows is that we are the sum of our experiences, and these experiences, good, bad or indifferent are profoundly impacted by the people with whom we surround ourselves.

TAKE HOME TIPS/QUESTIONS

- **Think about all of the times when feelings you have had for ex-partners surfaced in subsequent relationships? What was/were the trigger(s)?**
- **How did this transference of feelings/emotions affect your subsequent relationship(s)?**
- **What might you be able to do to remove the transfer cues?**

2. How a White Bear Can Teach You to Forget Your Ex

Don't think of the white bear.

If you're like most people, you are now probably sitting in front of your tablet or book doing exactly what you were just instructed not to do—thinking of a white bear. In fact, you are probably fixating on the white bear. Certainly, if you weren't thinking of the white bear before, you are now.

This laser-like focus on the exact idea I instructed you to block out results from what researchers refer to as the ironic process theory, or more simply, the white bear effect. In an influential research study, participants were asked to verbalize their stream of consciousness and not think about a white bear. Despite these explicit instructions, not only did participants have difficulty suppressing thoughts of the forbidden white bear, but the white bear surfaced with an unusually high frequency.[1]

This idea relates to relationships as well. After breaking up with a significant other, you may make a conscious effort to avoid thinking about him/her. However, in doing that, you wind up focusing on your ex, which is exactly what you intended not to do in the first place.

A breakup can be an incredibly painful experience. Even if you are emotionally detached from your partner by the time you break up, you loved him/her at one point, and ending the relationship will typically cause you to experience a sense of loss. Importantly, there are many variables that can affect the amount of emotional distress you experience due to this loss, such as the quality and length of the newly ended relationship, as well as how you perceived that relationship.[2] For example, if you two were friends before becoming romantically involved, the loss of the relationship will be much more difficult to deal with.

So how can we forget about our ex and why do we care about white bears?

Basically, do not force yourself to avoid thinking about your ex, lest you fall prey to the classic white bear effect. While it is easy to get rid of tangible items, such as a gift or his/her sweatshirt, thoughts are more challenging to remove. If you make the conscious decision to not think about your ex, your former significant other is likely to invade your thoughts. It is best to keep busy and *naturally* distract yourself with other, more pleasant thoughts. More concretely, researcher Daniel M. Wegner suggests several therapeutic ideas for "setting the bears free."[3] These ideas are listed below, many of which may come in handy as you work on recovering from that prior relationship you just can't seem to forget about (no matter how hard you try). Some of the recommendations are contradictory to one another, because the techniques that work best vary from person to person.

- **Focused distraction-** Think of something else, such as a hobby or activity that you enjoy when your ex comes to mind. This will help by shifting focus to areas that may enable you cope with the breakup.
- **Stress and load avoidance-** Stress hinders your ability to suppress the unwanted thoughts. Try to avoid stressful situations if at all possible, especially those in which your ex is likely to be present.
- **Thought postponement-** It is easier to put off thinking about something on a temporary basis. Being overly ambitious and permanently suppressing a thought is likely to lead to failure.[3] Focus on avoiding your ex's social media accounts for a few days at a time, rather than permanently. This is much more manageable.
- **Acceptance and commitment-** This approach offers "...strategies for reducing the emotional impact of the thought by changing perspectives or adopting special approaches to the thought in the attempt to neutralize its affective charge."[3] Here, you don't force yourself to not think about your ex, but rather train yourself to handle these thoughts in a more effective way.

In closing, Wegner notes, "Many of these strategies entail thinking about and accepting unwanted thoughts rather than suppressing them—and so, setting free the bears."[3] So, go ahead, think about your ex, and in doing so, set him/her free.

TAKE HOME TIPS/QUESTIONS
- **For those dealing with a breakup, lean on your support system- talk to friends and family. Definitely don't bottle up your emotions.**
- **If thinking about an ex, try to channel your emotions in positive ways, by keeping busy with**

hobbies or extracurricular activities.
- Don't force yourself to completely forget the person, because doing so will only make it more challenging; instead, allow yourself to naturally grieve and heal.

3. Breaking Up Is Hard to Do

It is natural for you to experience anger as a result of the end of a relationship, and often this anger can help you to put the relationship and its demise into proper perspective. It can also serve as a motivating factor to assist you in moving on. Research has shown that individuals, especially those who are anxiously attached, are best able to move on from past partners when they have new relationships.[1]

Those who are anxiously attached often act very insecure in their relationships (even if they have no reason to be) and are constantly looking for reassurance. As a result, they cling to their partners. They may do this to allay their fears of being alone or because they need validation from their significant other.

Overall, they tend to maintain their ties to an ex-partner, because they are not confident about future relationship success. Research suggests that increasing optimism about future prospects will allow anxiously attached individuals to let go of their feelings for ex-partners.[1]

When it comes to handling the aftermath of a

relationship, it really depends on who was the "initiator" and who was the "partner" during the dissolution.[2] Breakups are rarely mutual; instead, each person has their own interpretation of the relationship's demise.

Based on Diane Vaughan's research[3] on the process of uncoupling, the initiator is the first person to express displeasure with the relationship and want out. He/she goes through the process of experiencing single life (and potentially finding another partner) from the secure base of the relationship. When the partner is finally clued in to the fact that the relationship is ending, he/she is usually taken by surprise. This makes the healing process much more difficult for the partner. Essentially, the initiator can enact preemptive strategies while in the current relationship to ease the transition from one partner to another, such as through finding someone new.

Research has shown that factors that lead to more pain in the aftermath of a breakup are commitment to the relationship, duration of the relationship and the length of time since the relationship has ended.[4] The emotional experience and healing also depend on how costly the end of the relationship was for people, which in turn may be a result of their age and/or what they were looking for at that time in their lives. If someone was just in it for the short term, the breakup will not be as difficult. If a person finds that he/she has a large pool of potential others to choose from (think of a high school or college student surrounded by many single individuals), then the breakup process will not be as painful.

Gender differences may also come into play. What we do know from emotion and gender research is that women tend to be more emotionally responsive as they are better at decoding others' emotions. Research also shows that women tend to be more empathetic and likely to express this empathy. It may be less about the differences between the genders, but rather how we express our emotions.

A lot of what we do see in terms of the differences

between men and women, may in fact be due to societal influences. Men are much more likely to repress the expression of emotion, which is something that society has ingrained in us. For example, think of the saying "Big boys don't cry." If a man was to call his friends up, crying about the end of a relationship, he would be treated very differently than a woman. Women, are encouraged to express their emotions and talk about their feelings, and as such, are better equipped for working through the pain and/or unresolved anger.

TAKE HOME TIPS/QUESTIONS

- How have you handled breakups in the past? What were some helpful strategies? Which actions/behaviors led to more pain?
- What might you be able to do to channel the anger, hurt, and pain when confronted with a difficult experience?
- Have you noticed gender differences when it comes to dealing with breakups? If so, what are they?

X. The Dark Side: Infidelity in Relationships

1. A "Double-Shot" of Cheating

The need to belong is a basic human drive.[1] Relationships are important for our well-being, and marital relationships serve as buffers against stress.[2] Marital quality is also associated with better health.[3] The benefits of being in a relationship, such as those just mentioned, may explain why people are often very resistant to break social bonds and experience strong negative emotions when they feel as if their relationships may be compromised.

Cheating (or being cheated on) is one of the most detrimental behaviors to the survival of a relationship. Infidelity shakes the ground upon which the relationship was built, as it creates a violation of trust and breaks the commitment each partner made to one another. Not only does the act of cheating create tension and potentially destroy the relationship, but the *perception* that a partner may be cheating is also problematic. If there is suspicion of infidelity, that alone can create a rift between the members of the couple. Therefore, it is important to know how people view cheating and what behaviors people believe violate the terms of a committed relationship.

In the famous paradigm used by Buss, Larsen, Westen,

and Semmelroth,[4] college-aged participants were forced to choose between two alternatives when asked, which behavior is more distressing: (a) your partner forming an emotional attachment with another individual; or (b) your partner having sex with this other individual. Females largely found the thought of their partner forming an emotional entanglement with another individual more painful, while males selected the sexual infidelity option as being more troublesome.

The Evolutionary Perspective

From an evolutionary perspective, this difference is due to the selection pressures placed on the individuals of each gender. Women fear that when a man has become emotionally involved with another person, these women may lose some of the resources they have secured from their male partners. The man, however, fears that if the woman is having sex outside of the relationship, he is expending his resources on kin that potentially are not his, and as such, paternity certainty becomes very important. Basically, both are weary of a circumstance in which their genetic offspring are not getting the resources needed.

Jealousy may have evolved as a result of the unique reproductive challenges that our ancestors faced.[5] Men, in particular, had to struggle with paternity certainty. Women, on the other hand, respond with jealousy when they suspect that the resources provided by their men and reserved for their offspring are being diverted elsewhere. Therefore, they would worry most when their mates develop emotional connections with others as this signals the potential to re-allocate the resources to new women.

An Alternative View

Not everyone agrees with this summary. Social-role theorists argue that the evolutionary-based argument is incorrect and the data are a result of the nature of the format in which the participants were polled. The "double-shot hypothesis" suggests that when forced to select an answer, participants will pick the infidelity choice they assume co-occurs with the other type of infidelity, meaning that they will choose the option that they feel incorporates the other.[6] Specifically, men make the assumption that for a woman to have sex with someone, she must have already fallen in love; women suspect that for a man to have fallen in love, he must have already had sex with that outsider. Once the forced choice was removed and participants were able to rate their views on infidelity on a continuous scale (a scale of 1 to 5 indicating how upsetting they found the infidelity to be), gender differences disappeared. This demonstrates that the differences may partially have been a result of the question format.

TAKE HOME TIPS/QUESTIONS

- **What do you think is more painful: sexual or emotional infidelity?**
- **What expectations do you have for your partner regarding fidelity?**
- **Schedule a time to have a discussion about faithfulness and expectations with your partner.**

2. Infidelity and Jealousy from an Evolutionary Perspective

When you feel as if someone poses a threat to your relationship (whether they do or not), jealousy likely creeps in. Researchers note that jealousy is characterized by fear of loss, distrust, or anger, as one is worried about losing a relationship due to a rival.[1] Essentially, jealousy serves as a mechanism by which the person remains hypervigilant to protect his/her relationship from potential intruders. One common scenario which can elicit jealousy is when your partner is in the presence of available and datable others, resulting in the sense that he/she may be unfaithful.

Infidelity

In the previous chapter, I discussed theories of infidelity, focusing on the different perspectives offered by evolutionary psychologists and social-role theorists. The dispute between these two perspectives focuses on the difference in how distress is measured. One approach is to use "forced choice" alternatives, which include answer choices in which a participant is to pick which is more upsetting from two pre-selected responses: your partner forming an emotional attachment with another individual (emotional infidelity) or your partner having sex with this other individual (sexual infidelity). Evolutionary psychologists have used this forced-choice paradigm to show that men are more upset by sexual infidelity, while women are more distressed by emotional infidelity.[2]

From an evolutionary psychological perspective, the gender differences in outcomes resulting from an unfaithful partner, lead to different reactions to infidelity.[1] As previously mentioned, women fear that when a man has become emotionally involved with another, they (the women who have been cheated on) may lose some of the resources they have secured from their male partners. Men, however, fear that if their female partners are having sex outside of the relationship, the men are expending their resources on kin that potentially are not theirs. Basically both are weary of a circumstance in which their genetic offspring are not getting the resources needed.

Not everyone agrees with the evolutionary perspective and instead feel that the gender differences are merely a result of the way in which the cheating scenarios are presented. Researchers in opposition to the evolutionary perspective note that gender differences disappear when participants can rate their views on a continuous scale.[3] When forced to select an answer, people will choose the type (sexual or emotional) that co-occurs with the other.[3] In relating this to the choice women make (emotional infidelity is more distressing), it is thought that a woman will assume that if her husband has fallen in love, he has already had sex with the other woman. Therefore, the selection encompasses both types of infidelity.

Infidelity and Jealousy

Extending the evolutionary perspective further, jealousy may have evolved as a result of the reproductive challenges (e.g., not having enough resources to provide for the child) that our ancestors faced and the issues that would arise if a partner is unfaithful.[4] Men, in particular, have to struggle with paternity certainty, or the fact that they can't be completely sure whether the child a pregnant woman is carrying is his or another man's. Men would need to respond with jealousy if they suspected that their mate was about to stray, as this would decrease the likelihood that the woman would have sexual relations with another man. Women, on the other hand, respond with jealousy when they suspect that the resources provided by their male partners, and reserved for their offspring, are being diverted elsewhere.

What Does the Research Say?

One researcher conducted an experiment to examine the evolutionary perspective's accuracy.[4] In this study, the researcher manipulated the scenario (imagining your partner having sex or imagining your partner falling in love with someone else) and the race of the individuals (someone of the same or of a different race). If jealousy really arises from the need for the man to be certain of his paternity, sexual infidelity should be more threatening. Similarly, from the same perspective, women should find emotional infidelity more displeasing as it signals the re-allocation of necessary resources. The race of the person with whom the infidelity is committed should not influence the participants' responses, if the evolutionary perspective is the best explanation, as they are only concerned with paternity certainty or resources. However, if jealousy is a general emotional reaction to a potential threat to a relationship, then the race of the person with whom the partner is cheating may play a role. The researchers chose race as a variable to manipulate, as it is unrelated to the sex specific threat of infidelity.

For this study, 286 students, 214 females and 72 males, from Southeastern Louisiana University were presented with four scenarios in which their partner was unfaithful, based upon the manipulations dealing with type of infidelity and race. Participants also rated, on six 7-point scales, how angry, jealous, calm, threatened, relieved and hurt they felt in response to each scenario.

Researchers showed that the majority of men found imagining their partner's sexual infidelity with a member of the same race as more upsetting than emotional infidelity with a member of a different race. Along the same line, men were more upset when imagining their partner's sexual infidelity with a member of a different race than their partner's emotional infidelity with someone of the same race. Either way, for the men, sexual infidelity was always the worst scenario. The race of the person did not affect the decisions the male participants made. For women, the majority picked sexual infidelity as more upsetting, which is inconsistent with the evolutionary perspective. It is important to note that these findings, for the women, did not reach statistical significance.

Results demonstrated little effect of the influence of race of the partner with whom the infidelity occurred on reactions to imagined infidelity. The results partially supported the perspective that jealousy evolved for mate retention, because men were angrier and more hurt than women in response to sexual rather than emotional infidelity. However, results were inconsistent with this in that they failed to show that women were more upset and hurt by emotional infidelity, compared to men. Overall, "women reported more anger over sexual than over emotional infidelity and were equally hurt by sexual and emotional infidelity."[3] Therefore, the idea that jealousy evolved specifically for mate retention is compelling, but does not account for all of the data.

Infidelity shakes the ground upon which the relationship is built, as it creates a violation of trust and breaks the commitment each partner made to one another. While this is clear, the theory best suited to explain our reactions to it is not.

TAKE HOME TIPS/QUESTIONS
- When have you experienced jealousy in your relationship? Why?
- If you experience jealousy, what might you be able to do to alleviate it? Plan to have a discussion with your partner.

XI. Steps for Success: Keys for Long, Lasting, and Loving Relationships

1. Combating the Four Horsemen

Conflict is an inevitable part of any relationship. While those in healthy relationships try to avoid fighting, a couple simply cannot get away without arguing every now and then. In fact, conflict isn't always detrimental, as it can lead to growth and change within relationships. Most of the arguments couples have are trivial (e.g. who left the dishes in the sink without cleaning them), but it is the way in which we argue that can make or break a couple.

John Gottman, renowned psychologist, is famous for discussing healthy and unhealthy relationship patterns, and specifically has focused a great deal of his research on what he coins the "four horsemen of the apocalypse."[1] These four horsemen are so detrimental because they are antithetical to what makes relationships thrive. They also lead to the escalation of negativity in interactions with your partner. It is this escalation of negative communication that predicts divorce.

The four horsemen are:

1. **Criticism-** attacking your partner's character.

Relating back to our previous example, a person who criticizes may say, "You always leave the dishes in the sink, because you are such a slob." Criticism is always directed at the person, rather than the behavior and can be very hurtful.

2. **Defensiveness-** when a person, rather than taking responsibility for his/her actions, calls his/her partner out on something else. For example, rather than owning that you left the dishes in the sink, you say, "What did you expect me to do? I was running late, because you took forever getting ready in the bathroom this morning." When you get defensive, you avoid taking any responsibility for the problem.

3. **Contempt-** saying something hurtful, while coming from a place of superiority. Relating this to the presented example, you may say, "Of course you didn't get the promotion you wanted, you're a mess and can't even get it together at home." Contempt is so detrimental, because it conveys disrespect for your partner and is fueled by long-term negative thoughts that have been simmering below the surface.

4. **Stonewalling-** involves one person checking out, and 85% of the time it's the husband. For example, the wife may be arguing and expressing her feelings, however the husband is standing in front of her as if he is listening, but not processing anything she is saying. He has flooded and can no longer process her arguments. When stonewalling, a person may either walk away or just clam up and shut down in the middle of an argument, and as such, no productive resolution can be found. Also, by turning away from one another, you are not only avoiding the fight, but avoiding the marriage.

So now that we know what the four horsemen are, how can we interrupt them?

Below are the antidotes to the four horsemen.[2]

1. **Soft startup-** Rather than engage in criticism, it is better to use a soft startup during an argument. For example, describe your needs rather than calling out your partner. "I need you to clean the dishes in the morning, so the sink isn't a mess when I get to it." Or, "I feel frustrated when the sink is a mess and I can't even put anything else in there." Talk about your feelings and needs using "I" language.
2. **Accept responsibility-** Rather than getting defensive about what your partner has brought up, it is important to acknowledge when you have done something wrong.
3. **Build a culture of appreciation and respect-** Focus on something positive, rather than cutting your partner down. For example, "I appreciate that you helped with the laundry."
4. **Let your partner know that you are flooded and need a break-** It is important to decrease your physiological arousal level during a fight so you can have a productive conversation. A 20-minute break is often what is needed. During this time, it is important to do something that will soothe you.

Remember, it is not the couple that fights that is destined to break up. It is how the couple fights and handles disagreements that can lead to problems. You know how you tend to handle situations and if you intentionally try to "throw the last punch" to get your point across. Be aware of how you handle difficult situations and how you approach your partner. Also, make sure to avoid common traps that couples fall into when it comes to communication. Being aware of the four horsemen is a great first step.

TAKE HOME TIPS/QUESTIONS

- Spend some time thinking about how you relate to others when you get angry. Which of the four horsemen do you tend to use during an argument?
- Think about an argument you recently had. Jot down examples of the four horsemen as they relate to this argument and then write down the antidote to each.

2. The Shape of Love and Filling Our Tank

Robert Sternberg's triangular theory[1] provides a comprehensive discussion of the three components of love. The three components are intimacy, which involves sharing and honest communication; passion, which involves physiological arousal and desire; and commitment, which is maintaining that love over time. Sternberg notes that "[t]he amount of love one experiences depends on the absolute strength of these three components, and the kind of love one experiences depends on their strengths relative to each other."[1] Each of these components represents a point in a triangle, thus creating the triangular theory. The more love that is experienced, the greater the area of the triangle. The actual shape of the triangle is determined by which components are emphasized. If all are emphasized equally, the triangle is balanced. However, if one component is favored over the others (e.g. intimacy), you may wind up with a triangle that is skewed to the right, left, or isosceles.

We also have two triangles, our "real" and "ideal." If

our triangles overlap, our expectations have been met, which leads to romantic satisfaction. Conversely, if the triangles do not overlap, we experience dissatisfaction. According to Sternberg, different stages of the relationship can be explained by different combinations of the three components, but rather than get into the stages of a relationship, I would like to focus on how to maintain an overall loving relationship with our partners.

So how is it that we experience satisfaction and love within our relationships? I have read countless books discussing ways to keep both you and your partner satisfied, as well as real life accounts of couples discussing their relationships. However, one of the most widely quoted and popular books is New York Times best seller, *The 5 Love Languages: The Secret to Love That Lasts*,[2] written by Gary Chapman. Dr. Chapman is a relationship counselor, hosts a nationally syndicated radio program on marriage, and holds M.R.E. and Ph.D. degrees from Southwestern Baptist Theological Seminary.[3]

The goal of his book is to help readers understand ways to keep their "love tank full." I know, it's challenging to read this term without picturing Orange County Real Housewife Vicki Gunvalson lamenting about the emptiness of her love tank during an earlier season. Before you dismiss his ideas as a pop psychology fad or relationship-lite fluff, confirmatory factor analysis has shown that this five factor model does in fact have psychometric validity, compared to other unidimensional or three- or four-factor models.[4] It is important to note, however, that a scale that fits this model has not been created.

Chapman states that our love tanks remain full when we understand what our love language is, as well as the love language of our partner.

His love languages are the following:

1. **Words of affirmation-** is sending encouraging messages to your partner such as "I love you, because of what a good mother/father you are to our children."
2. **Quality time-** involves time spent together and giving your partner your undivided attention.
3. **Receiving gifts-** is giving physical tokens of appreciation and affection. This should not be confused with materialism, because the price is not important. The thought behind the gift is what matters.
4. **Acts of service-** is helping your partner with tasks and easing the burden of his/her responsibilities.
5. **Physical touch-** is creating closeness, which can be anything from hand holding to a massage to sexual intercourse.[2]

It is important when focusing on your partner, not to employ *your* love languages, but rather the one that meets your partner's needs.

While Chapman's book does not contain any experimental research, the ideas are wildly popular, mostly because they make a great deal of sense. In examining how your needs are met, and the ways to reach your partner, you get to learn a bit more about each other and your relationship, which at the end of the day is what growth in a relationship is really about, isn't it?

TAKE HOME TIPS/QUESTIONS
- **What is your love language?**
- **What do you think is your partner's love language?**
- **Create a list that can be useful to fill both your love tank and your partner's love tank.**

XII. The Power of Love: Concluding Thoughts and Final Remarks

1. Conclusion

Relationships are an important part of our everyday lives. Not only do they confer health benefits, but they increase our overall sense of well-being. The desire for affiliation and intimacy are two of the most basic human needs, which can be fulfilled by connections with close friends, family, or romantic partners. No matter what type of relationship, it should be characterized by a sense of support and strength.

The goal of this book was to present information about romantic relationships from their inception to potential demise, in an easy-to-understand, yet scientific manner. Using psychological principles and systematic observations, researchers have learned a great deal about the science of love and what contributes to healthy and fulfilling relationships.

I urge you to take the information presented in this book and apply it to your everyday life through an increased awareness of the underlying scientific processes involved in mate selection and relationship maintenance. I hope that this book has provided you with useful information that can give you a better glimpse into the mental processes and behaviors involved in human bonding.

I wish you all a great deal of success, happiness, and most importantly, love.

XIII. Footnotes

I.1
[1] Baumeister, R., & Leary, M. (1995). The need to belong: Desire for interpersonal attachment as a fundamental human motivation. *Psychological Bulletin, 117*, 497-529.

[2] Stutzer, A., & Frey, B. S. (2006). Does marriage make people happy, or do happy people get married? *The Journal of Socio-Economics, 35*(2), 326-347.

[3] Maestripieri, D., Klimczuk, A. C .E., Seneczko, M., Traficonte, D. M., & Wilson, M. C. (2013). Relationship status and relationship instability, but not dominance, predict individual differences in baseline cortisol levels. *PLoS ONE, 8*(12), e84003. doi:10.1371/journal.pone.0084003

[4] Kiecolt-Glaser, J. K., & Newton, T. L. (2001). Marriage and health: His and hers. *Psychological Bulletin, 127*, 472–503.

[5] Robles, T. F., Slatcher, R. B., Trombello, J. M., & McGinn, M. M. (2014). Marital quality and health: A meta-analytic review. *Psychological Bulletin, 140*(1), 140-187.

[6] Diener, E., Gohm, C. L., Suh, E., & Oishi, S. (2000). Similarity of the relations between marital status and subjective well-being across cultures. *Journal of Cross-Cultural Psychology, 31*(4), 419-436.

[7]Rohner, R. P., Khaleque, A., & Cournoyer, D. E. (2004). Cross-national perspectives on parental acceptance-rejection theory. *Marriage & Family Review, 35*(3-4), 85-105.

II.1

[1]Catron, M. L. (2015, January 9). To fall in love with anyone, do this. *The New York Times*. Retrieved from http://www.nytimes.com/2015/01/11/fashion/modern-love-to-fall-in-love-with-anyone-do-this.html?_r=0

[2]Aron, A., Melinat, E., Aron, A. N., Vallone, R. D., & Bator, R. J. (1997). The experimental generation of interpersonal closeness: A procedure and some preliminary findings. *Personality and Social Psychology Bulletin, 23*(4), 363-377.

II.2

[1]Datascience@Berkeley Blog. (2014, February 10). Big data seeks online love [Infographic]. Retrieved from https://d2jm4qw7 a11yde.cloudfront.net/blog/wp-content/uploads/2014/02/BigData-Dating-IG.jpg

[2]Smith, A., & Duggan, M. (2013). Online dating and relationships. Pew Research Center. Retrieved from http://www.pewinternet.org/2013/10/21/online-dating-relationships/

[3]Heino, R. D., Ellison, N. B., & Gibbs, J. L. (2010). Relationshopping: Investigating the market metaphor in online dating. *Journal of Social and Personal Relationships, 27*, 427–447. doi:10.1177/0265407510361614

[4]Fiore, A. T., & Donath, J. S. (2004). Online personals: An overview. *Computer Human Interaction*, 1395-1398.

[5]Finkel, E. J., Eastwick, P. W., Karney, B. R., Reis, H. T., & Sprecher, S. (2012). Online dating: A critical analysis from the perspective of psychological science. *Psychological Science in the Public Interest, 13*, 3–66. doi:10.1177/1529100612436522

[6]OKCupid. (2015). Match percentage. Retrieved from http://www.okcupid.com/help/match-percentages

III.1

[1]Backus, P. (2010). Why I don't have a girlfriend: An application of the Drake Equation to love in the UK. Retrieved from http://www2.warwick.ac.uk/fac/soc/economics/staff/pbackus/girlfriend/why_i_dont_have_a_girlfriend.pdf

[2]SETI Institute. (2016). The Drake Equation. Retrieved from http://www.seti.org/drakeequation

[3] NYC Department of City Planning. (2016). Current population estimates. Retrieved from http://www1.nyc.gov/site/planning/data-maps/nyc-population/current-future-populations.page

[4] Fry, H. (2015). *The mathematics of love*. New York: Simon & Schuster.

III.2

[1] Schwartz, B. (2004). *The paradox of choice*. New York: HarperCollins Publishers.

[2] Birch, J. (2016, February 3). Why you should break this common millennial dating habit. *Brit & Co*. Retrieved from http://www.brit.co/psychological-effect-of-yo-yo-dating/

[3] Lisitsa, E. (2013). Apply the research: Building your emotional bank account. The Gottman Institute. Retrieved from https://www.gottman.com/blog/apply-the-research-building-your-emotional-bank-account/

IV.1

[1] Fink, B., & Penton-Voak, I. (2002). Evolutionary psychology of facial attractiveness. *Current Directions in Psychological Science, 11*, 154-158.

[2] Pallet, P. M., Link, S., & Lee, K. (2010). New "golden" ratios of facial beauty. *Vision Research, 50*, 149-154.

[3] Fullard, W., & Reiling, A. M. (1976). An investigation of Lorenz's "babyness." *Child Development, 47*, 1191-1193.

[4] Korthase, M., & Trenholme, I. (1982). Perceived age and perfective physical attractiveness. *Perceptual and Motor Skills, 54*, 1251-1258.

[5] Cunningham, M. R. (1986). Measuring the physical in physical attractiveness: Quasi-experiments on the sociobiology of female facial beauty. *Journal of Personality and Social Psychology, 50*(5), 925-935. doi:10.1037/0022-3514.50.5.925

IV.2

[1] Cunningham, M. R. (1986). Measuring the physical in physical attractiveness: Quasi-experiments on the sociobiology of female facial beauty. *Journal of Personality and Social Psychology, 50*(5), 925-935. doi:10.1037/0022-3514.50.5.925

[2] American Psychological Association. (2007). Report of the APA task force on the sexualization of girls. *American Psychological Association*. Retrieved from http://www.apa.org/pi/women/programs/girls/report-summary.pdf

[3] O'Donohue, W., Gold, S. R., & McKay, J. S. (1997). Children as sexual objects: Historical and gender trends in magazines. *Sexual Abuse: Journal of Research & Treatment, 9*, 291-301.

[4]National Sexual Violence Resource Center. (2015). What is healthy sexuality and consent? Retrieved from http://www.nsvrc.org/sites/default/files/saam_2015_what-is-healthy-sexuality-and-consent.pdf

[5]Fredrickson, B. L., & Roberts, T. A. (1997). Objectification theory: Toward understanding women's lived experience and mental health risks. *Psychology of Women Quarterly, 21*,173-206.

[6]Tree Change Dolls®. (n.d.). Retrieved from http://treechangedolls.tumblr.com/

[7]SBS2Australia. (2015, February 10). *Tree Change Dolls* [Video file]. Retrieved from https://youtu.be/lG-7e1vaB18

V.1

[1]Park, L. E., Young, A. F., & Eastwick, P. W. (2015). (Psychological) distance makes the heart grow fonder: Effects of psychological distance and relative intelligence on men's attraction to women. *Social Psychology Bulletin, 41*(11), 1459-1473.

[2]Buston, P. M., & Emlen, S. T. (2003). Cognitive processes underlying human mate choice: The relationship between self-perception and mate preference in Western society. *Proceedings of the National Academy of Sciences, 100*, 8805-8810.

[3]Cohen, M. T., & Wilson, K. (2015, March). The relationship between mate selection preferences and academic motivation. Poster presented at the 2015 Annual Meeting of the Eastern Psychological Association, Philadelphia, PA.

[4]Tesser, A. (1988). Toward a self-evaluation maintenance model of social behavior. *Advances in Experimental Social Psychology, 21*, 181-228.

[5]Ratliff, K. A., & Oishi, S. (2013). Gender differences in implicit self-esteem following a romantic partner's success or failure. *Journal of Personality and Social Psychology, 105*(4), 688-702.

[6]Collins, N. L. (1996). Working models of attachment: Implications for explanation, emotion, and behavior. *Journal of Personality and Social Psychology, 71*, 810-832.

V.2

[1]Kurzban, R., & Weeden, J. (2005). HurryDate: Mate preferences in action. *Evolution and Human Behavior, 26*, 227-44.

[2]McFarland, D. A., Jurafsky D., & Rawlings, C. (2013). Making the connection: Social bonding in courtship situations. *American Journal of Sociology, 118*(6), 1596-1649.

[3]Grammer, K. (1989). Human courtship behavior: Biological basis and cognitive processing. In A. E. Rasa, C. Vogel & E. Voland (Eds.), *The sociobiology of sexual and reproductive strategies* (pp. 147-169). New York: Chapmann and Hall.

[4]Eaton, A. A., & Rose, S. (2011). Has dating become more egalitarian? A 35 year review using sex roles. *Sex Roles, 64*(11/12), 843-862.

[5]Cohen, M. T. (2016). It's not you, it's me…No, actually it's you: Perceptions of what makes a first date successful or not. *Sexuality and Culture, 20*(1), 173-191.

VI.1

[1]Zhang, Y., & Epley, N. (2012). Exaggerated, mispredicted, and misplaced: When 'it's the thought that counts' in gift exchanges. *Journal of Experimental Psychology: General, 141*(4), 667-681.

[2]Clarke, J. R. (2006). Different to 'dust collectors'? The giving and receiving of experience gifts. *Journal of Consumer Behaviour, 5*(6), 533-549.

[3]Van Boven, L., & Gilovich, T. (2003). To do or to have? That is the question. *Journal of Personality and Social Psychology, 85*(6), 1193-1202

VI.2

[1]MissPiggyFans.com. (2005). *Miss Piggy and Kermit the Frog*. Retrieved from http://www.misspiggyfans.com/Kermit/

[2]Walster, E., Walster, G. W., Piliavin, J., & Schmidt, L. (1973). 'Playing hard to get': Understanding an elusive phenomenon. *Journal of Personality and Social Psychology, 26*(1), 113-121. doi:10.1037/h0034234

[3]Harris, P. (Director). (1976, November 27). The Muppet Show- Candice Bergen. [Television series episode]. Borehamwood, Hertfordshire, England, UK: Incorporated Television Company.

VII.1

[1]Dutton, D. G., & Aron, A. P. (1974). Some evidence for heightened sexual attraction under conditions of high anxiety. *Journal of Personality and Social Psychology, 30*, 510–517.

[2]Baumeister, R. F., & Bushman, B. J. (2008). *Social Psychology & Human Nature*. Belmont, CA: Thomson Wadsworth.

[3]Cohen, B., Waugh, G., & Place, K. (1989). At the movies: An unobtrusive study of arousal-attraction. *The Journal of Social Psychology, 129*, 691-693.

[4]Meston, C. M., & Frohlich, P. F. (2003). Love at first fright: Partner salience moderates roller-coaster-induced excitation transfer. *Archives of Sexual Behavior, 32*(6), 537-544.

VII.2

[1]Williams, R. M., & Francken, J. C. (2012). Embodied cognition: Taking the next step. *Frontiers In Psychology, 3*, 1-3.

[2]Zhong, C., & Leonardelli, G. J. (2008). Cold and lonely: Does social exclusion literally feel cold? *Psychological Science, 19*, 838-842.
[3]Hong, J., & Sun, Y. (2012). Warm it up with love: The effect of physical coldness on liking of romance movies. *Journal of Consumer Research, 39*(2), 293-306.

VIII.1

[1]Rinaldi, R. (2015). *The wild oats project: One woman's midlife quest for passion at any cost.* New York: Sarah Crichton Books.
[2]Conley, T. D., Moors, A. C., Matsick, J. L., & Ziegler, A. (2013). The fewer the merrier?: Assessing stigma surrounding consensually non-monogamous romantic relationships. *Analyses of Social Issues and Public Policy (ASAP), 13*(1), 1-30. doi:10.1111/j.1530-2415.2012.01286.x
[3]Hosking, W. (2013). Satisfaction with open sexual agreements in Australian gay men's relationships: The role of perceived discrepancies in benefit. *Archives of Sexual Behavior, 42*(7), 1309-1317. doi:10.1007/s10508-012-0005-9
[4]Zimmerman, K. J. (2012). Clients in sexually open relationships: Considerations for therapists. *Journal of Feminist Family Therapy: An International Forum, 24*(3), 272-289.
[5]Savage, D. (2014, May 5). Monogam-Ish Relationships, From Dan Savage [Video file]. Retrieved from http://www.huffingtonpost.com/2014/05/02/monogamish-relationships-_n_5255297.html
[6]Thompson, B. (Producer), & Collier, D. (Director). (1993). *For better or for worse* [Film Documentary]. United States: Studio B Films.
[7]Glass, S. P. & Wright, T. M. (1985). Sex differences in type of extramarital involvement and marital satisfaction. *Sex Roles, 12*, 1101-1120.
[8]Finn, M. D., Tunariu, A. D., & Lee, K. C. (2012). A critical analysis of affirmative therapeutic engagements with consensual non-monogamy. *Sexual and Relationship Therapy, 27*(3), 205-216. doi:10.1080/14681994.2012.702893

VIII.2

[1]Conley, T. D., Moors, A. C., Matsick, J. L., & Ziegler, A. (2013). The fewer the merrier?: Assessing stigma surrounding consensually non-monogamous romantic relationships. *Analyses of Social Issues and Public Policy (ASAP), 13*, 1-30. doi:10.1111/j.1530-2415.2012.01286.x
[2]Graham, N. (2014). Polyamory: A call for increased mental health professional awareness. *Archives of Sexual Behavior, 43*(6), 1031-1034.

[3]Brandon, M. (2011). The challenge of monogamy: Bringing it out of the closet and into the treatment room. *Sexual and Relationship Therapy, 26*(3), 271-277. doi:10.1080/14681994.2011.574114

[4]Mitchell, M. E., Bartholomew, K., & Cobb, R. J. (2014). Need fulfillment in polyamorous relationships. *Journal of Sex Research, 51*(3), 329-339.

[5]Modern Poly. (n.d.). Polyamory group registry. Retrieved from http://web.archive.org/web/20141218060256/http://polygroups.com/

[6]Manley, M. H., Diamond, L. M., & van Anders, S. M. (2015). Polyamory, monoamory, and sexual fluidity: A longitudinal study of identity and sexual trajectories. *Psychology of Sexual Orientation and Gender Diversity, 2*(2), 168-180.

[7]Klesse, C. (2011). Notions of love in polyamory- Elements in a discourse on multiple loving. *Laboratorium, 3*, 4–25. Retrieved from http://www.soclabo.org/index.php/laboratorium/article/view/250/586

[8]Easton, D. & Hardy, J. W. (2009). The ethical slut: A practical guide to polyamory, open relationships & other adventures (2nd edition). New York: Crown Publishing Group.

IX.1

[1]Levy, K. N., & Scala, J. W. (2012). Transference, transference interpretations, and transference-focused psychotherapies. *Psychotherapy, 49*, 391-403. doi:10.1037/a0029371

[2]Transference [Def. 2]. (n.d.). In *Merriam-Webster.com*. Retrieved from http://www.merriam-webster.com/dictionary/transference

[3]Andersen, S., & Berk, M. (1998). The social-cognitive model of transference: Experiencing past relationships in the present. *Current Directions in Psychological Science, 7*, 109-115.

[4]Andersen, S. M., & Przybylinski, E. (2012). Experiments on transference in interpersonal relations: Implications for treatment. *Psychotherapy, 49*(3), 370-383. doi:10.1037/a0029116

IX.2

[1]Wegner, D. M., Schneider, D. J., Carter, S., & White, L. (1987). Paradoxical effects of thought suppression. *Journal of Personality and Social Psychology, 53*, 5–13.

[2]Sprecher, S., Felmlee, D., Metts, S., Fehr, B., & Vanni, D. (1998). Factors associated with distress following the breakup of a close relationship. *Journal of Social and Personal Relationships, 15*(6), 791-809.

[3]Wegner, D. M. (2011). Setting free the bears: Escape from thought suppression. *American Psychologist, 66*(8), 671-680.

IX.3

[1] Spielmann, S. S., MacDonald, G., & Wilson, A. E. (2009). On the rebound: Focusing on someone new helps anxiously attached individuals let go of ex-partners. *Personality and Social Psychology Bulletin, 35*, 1382-1394.

[2] Felmlee, D. H. (2001). From appealing to appalling: Disenchantment with a romantic partner. *Sociological Perspectives, 44*(3), 263-280.

[3] Vaughan, D. (1986). *Uncoupling: Turning points in intimate relationships.* New York: Oxford University Press.

[4] Sprecher, S., Felmlee, D., Metts, S., Fehr, B., & Vanni, D. (1998). Factors associated with distress following the breakup of a close relationship. *Journal of Social and Personal Relationships, 15*(6), 791-809.

X.1

[1] Baumeister, R., & Leary, M. (1995). The need to belong: Desire for interpersonal attachment as a fundamental human motivation. *Psychological Bulletin, 117*, 497-529.

[2] Maestripieri, D., Klimczuk, A. C. E., Seneczko, M., Traficonte, D. M., & Wilson, M. C. (2013). Relationship status and relationship instability, but not dominance, predict individual differences in baseline cortisol levels. *PLoS ONE, 8*(12), e84003. doi:10.1371/journal.pone.0084003

[3] Kiecolt-Glaser, J. K., & Newton, T. L. (2001). Marriage and health: His and hers. *Psychological Bulletin, 127*, 472–503.

[4] Buss, D. M. (2000). The dangerous passion: Why jealousy is as necessary as love and sex. New York: Free Press.

[5] Bassett, J. F. (2005). Sex differences in jealousy in response to a partner's imagined sexual or emotional infidelity with a same or different race other. *North American Journal of Psychology, 7*(1), 71-84.

[6] DeSteno, D. & Salovey, P. (1996). Evolutionary origins of sex differences in jealousy: Questioning the "fitness" of the model. *Psychological Science, 7*, 367-372.

X.2

[1] Parrot, W. G., & Smith, R. H. (1993) Distinguishing the experiences of envy and jealousy. *Journal of Personality and Social Psychology, 64*, 906-920.

[2] Buss, D. M. (2000). *The dangerous passion: Why jealousy is as necessary as love and sex.* New York: Free Press.

[3] DeSteno, D. & Salovey, P. (1996). Evolutionary origins of sex differences in jealousy: Questioning the "fitness" of the model. *Psychological Science, 7*, 367-372.

[4]Bassett, J. F. (2005). Sex differences in jealousy in response to a partner's imagined sexual or emotional infidelity with a same or different race other. *North American Journal of Psychology, 7*(1), 71-84.

XI.1

[1]Gottman, J., & Silver, N. (1999). *The seven principles for making marriage work*. New York: Three Rivers Press.

[2]Lisitsa, E. (2013). The four horsemen: The antidotes. Retrieved from: https://www.gottman.com/blog/the-four-horsemen-the-antidotes/

XI.2

[1]Sternberg, R. J. (1986). A triangular theory of love. *Psychological Review, 93*(2), 119-135.

[2]Chapman, G. D. (2010). *The 5 love languages: The secret to love that lasts.* Chicago: Northfield Publishing.

[3]The 5 Love Languages. (2016). About Gary Chapman. Retrieved from http://www.5lovelanguages.com/about/gary-chapman/

[4]Egbert, N., & Polk, D. (2006). Speaking the language of relational maintenance: A validity test of Chapman's (1992) five love languages. *Communication Research Reports, 23*(1), 19-26.

XIV. References

Allen, K. (1995). Coping with life changes and transitions: The role of pets. *Interactions, 13*(3), 5–8.

American Psychological Association. (2007). Report of the APA task force on the sexualization of girls. *American Psychological Association.* Retrieved from http://www.apa.org/pi/women/programs/girls/report-summary.pdf

Andersen, S., & Berk, M. (1998). The social-cognitive model of transference: Experiencing past relationships in the present. *Current Directions in Psychological Science, 7*, 109-115.

Andersen, S. M., & Przybylinski, E. (2012). Experiments on transference in interpersonal relations: Implications for treatment. *Psychotherapy, 49*(3), 370-383. doi:10.1037/a0029116

Archuleta, K. L., Grable, J. E., & Britt, S. L. (2013). Financial and relationship satisfaction as a function of harsh start-up and shared goals and values. *Journal of Financial Counseling and Planning, 24*(1), 3-14.

Aron, A., Melinat, E., Aron, A. N., Vallone, R. D., & Bator, R. J. (1997). The experimental generation of interpersonal closeness: A procedure and some preliminary findings. *Personality and Social Psychology Bulletin, 23*(4), 363-377.

Avivi, Y. E., Laurenceau, J-P., & Carver, C. S. (2009). Linking relationship quality to perceived mutuality of relationship goals and perceived goal progress. *Journal of Social and Clinical Psychology, 28*, 137-164.

Backus, P. (2010). Why I don't have a girlfriend: An application of the Drake Equation to love in the UK. Retrieved from http://www2.warwick.ac.uk/fac/soc/economics/staff/pbackus/girlfriend/why_i_dont_have_a_girlfriend.pdf

Bassett, J. F. (2005). Sex differences in jealousy in response to a partner's imagined sexual or emotional infidelity with a same or different race other. *North American Journal of Psychology, 7*(1), 71-84.

Baumeister, R. F., & Bushman, B. J. (2008). *Social Psychology & Human Nature.* Belmont, CA: Thomson Wadsworth.

Baumeister, R., & Leary, M. (1995). The need to belong: Desire for interpersonal attachment as a fundamental human motivation. *Psychological Bulletin, 117,* 497-529.

Birch, J. (2016, February 3). Why you should break this common millennial dating habit. *Brit & Co.* Retrieved from http://www.brit.co/psychological-effect-of-yo-yo-dating/

Bleske-Rechek, A., Remiker, M. W., & Baker, J. P. (2009). Similar from the start: Assortment in young adult dating couples and its link to relationship stability over time. *Individual Differences Research, 7*(3), 142-158.

Botwin, M. D., Buss, D. M, & Shackelford, T. K. (1997). Personality and mate preferences: Five factors in mate selection and marital satisfaction. *Journal of Personality, 65*(1), 107-136.

Brandon, M. (2011). The challenge of monogamy: Bringing it out of the closet and into the treatment room. *Sexual and Relationship Therapy, 26*(3), 271-277. doi:10.1080/14681994.2011.574114

Buss, D. M. (1984). Marital assortment for personality dispositions: Assessment with three different data sources. *Behavior Genetics, 14,* 111–123.

Buss, D. M. (2000). The dangerous passion: Why jealousy is as necessary as love and sex. New York: Free Press.

Buston, P. M., & Emlen, S. T. (2003). Cognitive processes underlying human mate choice: The relationship between self-perception and mate preference in Western society. *Proceedings of the National Academy of Sciences, 100,* 8805-8810.

Catron, M. L. (2015, January 9). To fall in love with anyone, do this. *The New York Times.* Retrieved from http://www.nytimes.com/2015/01/11/fashion/modern-love-to-fall-in-love-with-anyone-do-this.html?_r=0

Chapman, G. D. (2010). *The 5 love languages: The secret to love that lasts.* Chicago: Northfield Publishing.

Clarke, J. R. (2006). Different to 'dust collectors'? The giving and receiving of experience gifts. *Journal of Consumer Behaviour, 5*(6), 533-549.

Cohen, B., Waugh, G., & Place, K. (1989). At the movies: An unobtrusive study of arousal-attraction. *The Journal of Social Psychology, 129*, 691-693.

Cohen, M. T. (2015, June 4). Features that signal attractiveness: The Kylie Jenner effect. *Science of Relationships*. Retrieved from http://www.scienceofrelationships.com/home/2015/6/4/features-that-signal-attractiveness-the-kylie-jenner-effect.html

Cohen, M. T. (2015, June 15). Is marriage really synonymous with monogamy? *Science of Relationships*. Retrieved from http://www.scienceofrelationships.com/home/2015/6/15/is-marriage-really-marriage-reallysynonymous-with-monogamy.html

Cohen, M. T. (2015, June 30). From Bratz to natural beauties. *Science of Relationships*. Retrieved from http://www.scienceofrelationships.com/home/2015/6/30/from-bratz-to-naturalbeauties.html

Cohen, M. T. (2015, July 22). "Clicking" with online dating. *Science of Relationships*. Retrieved from http://www.scienceofrelationships.com/home/2015/7/22/clicking-with-online-dating.html

Cohen, M. T. (2015, July 31). Creating closeness: In the lab and in real life. *Science of Relationships*. Retrieved from http://www.scienceofrelationships.com/home/2015/7/31/creating-closeness-in-the-lab-and-in-real-life.html

Cohen, M. T. (2015, August 6). Playing hard to get potentially fried this frog. *Science of Relationships*. Retrieved from http://www.scienceofrelationships.com/home/2015/8/6/playing-hard-to-get-potentially-fried-this-frog.html

Cohen, M. T. (2015, August 18). The ghost of relationships past. *Science of Relationships*. Retrieved from http://www.scienceofrelationships.com/home/2015/8/18/the-ghost-of-relationships-past.html

Cohen, M. T. (2015, August 25). Polyamory: Understanding relationship geometry. *Science of Relationships*. Retrieved from http://www.scienceofrelationships.com/home/2015/8/25/polyamory-understanding-relationship-geometry.html

Cohen, M. T. (2015, September 24). Misattribution in paradise: Would The Bachelor contestants have connected without all of the arousal inducing dates? *Science of Relationships*. Retrieved from http://www.scienceofrelationships.com/home/2015/9/24/misattribution-in-paradise-would-the-bachelor-contestants-ha.html

Cohen, M. T. (2015, October 1). A "double-shot" of cheating. *Science of Relationships*. Retrieved from http://www.scienceofrelationships.com/home/2015/10/1/a-double-shot-of-cheating.html

Cohen, M. T. (2015, December 8). Infidelity and jealousy from an evolutionary perspective. *Science of Relationships*. Retrieved from http://www.scienceofrelationships.com/home/2015/12/8/infidelity-and-jealousy-from-an-evolutionary-perspective.html

Cohen, M. T. (2016, February 2). Why do we watch romantic movies during winter storms? *Science of Relationships*. Retrieved from http://www.scienceofrelationships.com/home/2016/2/2/why-do-we-watch-romantic-movies-during-winter-storms.html

Cohen, M. T. (2016, February 5). Giving the gift of an experience this Valentine's Day. *Science of Relationships*. Retrieved from http://www.scienceof relationships.com /home/2016/2/5/ giving-the-gift-of-an-experience-this-valentines-day.html

Cohen, M. T. (2016). It's not you, it's me…No, actually it's you: Perceptions of what makes a first date successful or not. *Sexuality and Culture, 20*(1), 173-191. doi:10.1007/s12119-015-9322-1

Cohen, M. T. (2016). An exploratory study of individuals in non-traditional, alternative relationships: How "open" are we? *Sexuality and Culture, 20*(2), 295-315. doi:10.1007/s12119-015-9324-z

Cohen, M. T. (2016, May 8). How a white bear can teach you to forget your ex. *Science of Relationships*. Retrieved from http://www.scienceofrelationships.com/home/2016/5/8/how-a-white-bear-can-teach-you-to-forget-your-ex.html

Cohen, M. T., & Wilson, K. (2015, March). The relationship between mate selection preferences and academic motivation. Poster presented at the 2015 Annual Meeting of the Eastern Psychological Association, Philadelphia, PA.

Collins, N. L. (1996). Working models of attachment: Implications for explanation, emotion, and behavior. *Journal of Personality and Social Psychology, 71*, 810-832.

Conley, T. D., Moors, A. C., Matsick, J. L., & Ziegler, A. (2013). The fewer the merrier?: Assessing stigma surrounding consensually non-monogamous romantic relationships. *Analyses of Social Issues and Public Policy (ASAP), 13*(1), 1-30. doi:10.1111/j1530-2415.2012.01286.x

Connolly, J. A., & Johnson, A. M. (1996). Adolescents' romantic relationships and the structure and quality of their close interpersonal ties. *Personal Relationships, 3*(2), 185-195.

Cunningham, M. R. (1986). Measuring the physical in physical attractiveness: Quasi-experiments on the sociobiology of female facial beauty. *Journal of Personality and Social Psychology, 50*(5), 925-935. doi:10.1037/0022-3514.50.5.925

Datascience@Berkeley Blog. (2014, February 10). Big data seeks online love [Infographic]. Retrieved from https://d2jm4qw7a11yde.cloudfront.net/blog/wp-content/uploads/2014/02/BigData-Dating-IG.jpg

DeLamater, J., Hyde, J. S., & Fong, M. (2008). Sexual satisfaction in the seventh decade of life. *Journal of Sex & Marital Therapy, 34*, 439-454.

DeSteno, D. & Salovey, P. (1996). Evolutionary origins of sex differences in jealousy: Questioning the "fitness" of the model. *Psychological Science, 7*, 367-372.

Dew, J. (2011). Financial issues and relationship outcomes among cohabiting individuals. *Family Relations: An Interdisciplinary Journal of Applied Family Studies, 60*(2), 178-190.

Diamond, L. M., & Hicks, A. M. (2011). "It's the economy, honey!" Couples' blame attributions during the 2007-2009 economic crisis. *Personal Relationships, 19*(3), 586-600.

Diener, E., Gohm, C. L., Suh, E., & Oishi, S. (2000). Similarity of the relations between marital status and subjective well-being across cultures. *Journal of Cross-Cultural Psychology, 31*(4), 419-436.

Dutton, D. G., & Aron, A. P. (1974). Some evidence for heightened sexual attraction under conditions of high anxiety. *Journal of Personality and Social Psychology, 30*, 510–517.

Eaton, A. A., & Rose, S. (2011). Has dating become more egalitarian? A 35 year review using sex roles. *Sex Roles, 64*(11/12), 843-862.

Easton, D. & Hardy, J. W. (2009). The ethical slut: A practical guide to polyamory, open relationships & other adventures (2nd edition). New York: Crown Publishing Group.

Egbert, N., & Polk, D. (2006). Speaking the language of relational maintenance: A validity test of Chapman's (1992) five love languages. *Communication Research Reports, 23*(1), 19-26.

Felmlee, D. H. (2001). From appealing to appalling: Disenchantment with a romantic partner. *Sociological Perspectives, 44*(3), 263-280.

Fink, B., & Penton-Voak, I. (2002). Evolutionary psychology of facial attractiveness. *Current Directions in Psychological Science, 11*, 154-158.

Finkel, E. J., Eastwick, P. W., Karney, B. R., Reis, H. T., & Sprecher, S. (2012). Online dating: A critical analysis from the perspective of psychological science. *Psychological Science in the Public Interest, 13*, 3-66. doi:10.1177/1529100612436522

Finn, M. D., Tunariu, A. D., & Lee, K. C. (2012). A critical analysis of affirmative therapeutic engagements with consensual non-monogamy. *Sexual and Relationship Therapy, 27*(3), 205-216. doi:10.1080/14681994.2012.702893

Fiore, A. T., & Donath, J. S. (2004). Online personals: An overview. *Computer Human Interaction*, 1395-1398.

Fredrickson, B. L., & Roberts, T. A. (1997). Objectification theory: Toward understanding women's lived experience and mental health risks. *Psychology of Women Quarterly, 21*, 173-206.

Fry, H. (2015). *The mathematics of love.* New York: Simon & Schuster.

Fullard, W., & Reiling, A. M. (1976). An investigation of Lorenz's "babyness." *Child Development, 47*, 1191-1193.

Glass, S. P. & Wright, T. M. (1985). Sex differences in type of extramarital involvement and marital satisfaction. *Sex Roles, 12*, 1101-1120.

Gordon, A. M., & Chen, S. (2016). Do you get where I'm coming from? Perceived understanding buffers against the negative impact of conflict on relationship satisfaction. *Personality and Social Psychology, 110*(2), 239-260.

Gottman, J., & Silver, N. (1999). *The seven principles for making marriage work*. New York: Three Rivers Press.

Graham, N. (2014). Polyamory: A call for increased mental health professional awareness. *Archives of Sexual Behavior, 43*(6), 1031-1034.

Grammer, K. (1989). Human courtship behavior: Biological basis and cognitive processing. In A. E. Rasa, C. Vogel & E. Voland (Eds.), *The sociobiology of sexual and reproductive strategies* (pp. 147-169). New York: Chapmann and Hall.

Gunderson, P., & Ferrari, J. (2008). Forgiveness of sexual cheating in romantic relationships: Effects of discovery method, frequency of offense, and presence of apology. *North American Journal of Psychology, 10*, 1–14.

Harris, P. (Director). (1976, November 27). The Muppet Show- Candice Bergen. [Television series episode]. Borehamwood, Hertfordshire, England, UK: Incorporated Television Company.

Heino, R. D., Ellison, N. B., & Gibbs, J. L. (2010). Relationshopping: Investigating the market metaphor in online dating. *Journal of Social and Personal Relationships, 27*, 427–447. doi:10.1177/0265407510361614

Herbenick, D. (2012, December 17). Balancing time together vs. apart: Every relationship is a balance of time spent together and time spent alone. *Psychology Today*. Retrieved from https://www.psychologytoday.com/blog/the-pleasures-sex/201212/balancing-time-together-vs-apart

Hong, J., & Sun, Y. (2012). Warm it up with love: The effect of physical coldness on liking of romance movies. *Journal of Consumer Research, 39*(2), 293-306.

Hosking, W. (2013). Satisfaction with open sexual agreements in Australian gay men's relationships: The role of perceived discrepancies in benefit. *Archives of Sexual Behavior, 42*(7), 1309-1317. doi:10.1007/s10508-012-0005-9

Johnson, M. D., & Galambos, N. L. (2014). Paths to intimate relationship quality from parent-adolescent relations and mental health. *Journal of Marriage and Family, 76*(1), 145-160.

Kiecolt-Glaser, J. K., & Newton, T. L. (2001). Marriage and health: His and hers. *Psychological Bulletin, 127*, 472–503.

Klesse, C. (2011). Notions of love in polyamory- Elements in a discourse on multiple loving. *Laboratorium, 3*, 4–25. Retrieved from http://www.soclabo.org/index.php/laboratorium/article/view/250/586

Korthase, M., & Trenholme, I. (1982). Perceived age and perfective physical attractiveness. *Perceptual and Motor Skills, 54*, 1251-1258.

Kurzban, R., & Weeden, J. (2005). HurryDate: Mate preferences in action. *Evolution and Human Behavior, 26*, 227–44.

Lee, K., & Zvonkovie, A. M. (2014). Journeys to remain childless: A grounded theory examination of decision-making processes among voluntarily childless couples. *Journal of Social and Personal Relationships, 31*, 535-553. doi:10.1177/0265407514522891

Levy, K. N., & Scala, J. W. (2012). Transference, transference interpretations, and transference-focused psychotherapies. *Psychotherapy, 49*, 391-403. doi:10.1037/a0029371

Lisitsa, E. (2013). Apply the research: Building your emotional bank account. The Gottman Institute. Retrieved from https://www.gottman.com/blog/apply-the-research-building-your-emotional-bank-account/

Lisitsa, E. (2013). The four horsemen: The antidotes. Retrieved from: https://www.gottman.com/blog/the-four-horsemen-the-antidotes/

Maestripieri, D., Klimczuk, A. C. E., Seneczko, M., Traficonte, D. M., & Wilson, M. C. (2013). Relationship status and relationship instability, but not dominance, predict individual differences in baseline cortisol levels. *PLoS ONE, 8*(12), e84003. doi:10.1371/journal.pone.0084003

Manley, M. H., Diamond, L. M., & van Anders, S. M. (2015). Polyamory, monoamory, and sexual fluidity: A longitudinal study of identity and sexual trajectories. *Psychology of Sexual Orientation and Gender Diversity, 2*(2), 168-180.

McFarland, D. A., Jurafsky D., & Rawlings, C. (2013). Making the connection: Social bonding in courtship situations. *American Journal of Sociology, 118*(6), 1596-1649.

Meston, C. M., & Frohlich, P. F. (2003). Love at first fright: Partner salience moderates roller-coaster-induced excitation transfer. *Archives of Sexual Behavior, 32*(6), 537-544.

MissPiggyFans.com. (2005). *Miss Piggy and Kermit the Frog*. Retrieved from http://www.misspiggyfans.com/Kermit/

Mitchell, M. E., Bartholomew, K., & Cobb, R. J. (2014). Need fulfillment in polyamorous relationships. *Journal of Sex Research, 51*(3), 329-339.

Modern Poly. (n.d.). Polyamory group registry. Retrieved from https://web.archive.org/web/20141218060256/http://polygroups.com/

National Sexual Violence Resource Center. (2015). What is healthy sexuality and consent? Retrieved from http://www.nsvrc.org/sites/default/files/saam_2015_what-is-healthy-sexuality-and-consent.pdf

NYC Department of City Planning. (2016). Current population estimates. Retrieved from http://www.1.nyc.gov/site/planning/data-maps/nyc-population/current-future-populations.page

O'Donohue, W., Gold, S. R., & McKay, J. S. (1997). Children as sexual objects: Historical and gender trends in magazines. *Sexual Abuse: Journal of Research & Treatment, 9*, 291-301.

OKCupid. (2015). Match percentage. Retrieved from http://www.ok cupid.com/help/match-percentages

Pallet, P. M., Link, S., & Lee, K. (2010). New "golden" ratios of facial beauty. *Vision Research, 50*, 149–154.

Parish, W. L., Luo, Y., Stolzenberg, R. M., Laumann, E. O., Farrer, G., & Pan, S. (2007). Sexual practices and sexual satisfaction: A population based study of Chinese urban adults. *Archives of Sexual Behavior, 36*, 5–20.

Park, L. E., Young, A. F., & Eastwick, P. W. (2015). (Psychological) distance makes the heart grow fonder: Effects of psychological distance and relative intelligence on men's attraction to women. *Social Psychology Bulletin, 41*(11), 1459-1473.

Parrot, W. G., & Smith, R. H. (1993) Distinguishing the experiences of envy and jealousy. *Journal of Personality and Social Psychology, 64*, 906-920.

Ratliff, K. A., & Oishi, S. (2013). Gender differences in implicit self-esteem following a romantic partner's success or failure. *Journal of Personality and Social Psychology, 105*(4), 688-702.

Reiter, M. J., & Gee, C. B. (2008). Open communication and partner support in intercultural and interfaith romantic relationships: A relational maintenance approach. *Journal of Social and Personal Relationships, 25*(4), 539-559.

Rinaldi, R. (2015). *The wild oats project: One woman's midlife quest for passion at any cost*. New York: Sarah Crichton Books.

Robles, T. F., Slatcher, R. B., Trombello, J. M., & McGinn, M. M. (2014). Marital quality and health: A meta-analytic review. *Psychological Bulletin, 140*(1), 140-187.

Roggensack, K. E., & Sillars, A. (2014). Agreement and understanding about honesty and deception rules in romantic relationships. *Journal of Social and Personal Relationships, 31*, 178-199.

Rohner, R. P., Khaleque, A., & Cournoyer, D. E. (2004). Cross-national perspectives on parental acceptance-rejection theory. *Marriage & Family Review, 35*(3-4), 85-105.

Savage, D. (2014, May 5). Monogam-Ish Relationships, From Dan Savage [Video file]. Retrieved from http://www.huffingtonpost.com/2014/05/02/monogamish-relationships-_n_5255297.html

SBS2Australia. (2015, February 10). *Tree Change Dolls* [Video file]. Retrieved from https://youtu.be/lG-7e1vaB18

Schneider, D. (2011). Market earnings and household work: New tests of gender performance theory. *Journal of Marriage and Family, 73,* 845-860.

Schwartz, B. (2004). *The paradox of choice.* New York: HarperCollins Publishers.

SETI Institute. (2016). The Drake Equation. Retrieved from http://www.seti.org/drakeequation

Smith, A., & Duggan, M. (2013). Online dating and relationships. Pew Research Center. Retrieved from http://www.pewinternet.org/2013/10/21/online-dating-relationships/

Spielmann, S. S., MacDonald, G., & Wilson, A. E. (2009). On the rebound: Focusing on someone new helps anxiously attached individuals let go of ex-partners. *Personality and Social Psychology Bulletin, 35,* 1382-1394.

Sprecher, S., Felmlee, D., Metts, S., Fehr, B., & Vanni, D. (1998). Factors associated with distress following the breakup of a close relationship. *Journal of Social and Personal Relationships, 15*(6), 791-809.

Sternberg, R. J. (1986). A triangular theory of love. *Psychological Review, 93*(2), 119-135.

Stutzer, A., & Frey, B. S. (2006). Does marriage make people happy, or do happy people get married? *The Journal of Socio-Economics, 35*(2), 326-347.

Tesser, A. (1988). Toward a self-evaluation maintenance model of social behavior. *Advances in Experimental Social Psychology, 21,* 181-228.

The 5 Love Languages. (2016). About Gary Chapman. Retrieved from http://www.5lovelanguages.com/about/gary-chapman/

Thompson, B. (Producer), & Collier, D. (Director). (1993). *For better or for worse* [Film Documentary]. United States: Studio B Films.

Transference [Def. 2]. (n.d.). In *Merriam-Webster.com.* Retrieved from http://www.merriam-webster.com/dictionary/transference

Tree Change Dolls®. (n.d.). Retrieved from http://treechangedolls.tumblr.com/

Van Boven, L., & Gilovich, T. (2003). To do or to have? That is the question. *Journal of Personality and Social Psychology, 85*(6), 1193-1202.

Vaughan, D. (1986). *Uncoupling: Turning points in intimate relationships.* New York: Oxford University Press.

Walsh, F. (2009). Human-animal bonds II: The role of pets in family systems and family therapy. *Family Process, 48*(4), 481-499.

Walster, E., Walster, G. W., Piliavin, J., & Schmidt, L. (1973). 'Playing hard to get': Understanding an elusive phenomenon. *Journal of Personality and Social Psychology, 26*(1), 113-121. doi:10.1037/h0034234

Watson, D., Beer, A., & McDade-Montez, E. (2014). The role of active assortment in spousal similarity. *Journal of Personality, 82*(2), 116-129. doi:10.1111/jopy.12039

Wegner, D. M. (2011). Setting free the bears: Escape from thought suppression. *American Psychologist, 66*(8), 671-680.

Wegner, D. M., Schneider, D. J., Carter, S., & White, L. (1987). Paradoxical effects of thought suppression. *Journal of Personality and Social Psychology, 53*, 5–13.

Williems, R. M., & Francken, J. C. (2012). Embodied cognition: Taking the next step. *Frontiers In Psychology, 3,* 1-3.

Zhang, Y., & Epley, N. (2012). Exaggerated, mispredicted, and misplaced: When 'it's the thought that counts' in gift exchanges. *Journal of Experimental Psychology: General, 141*(4), 667-681.

Zhong, C., & Leonardelli, G. J. (2008). Cold and lonely: Does social exclusion literally feel cold? *Psychological Science, 19*, 838-842.

Zimmerman, K. J. (2012). Clients in sexually open relationships: Considerations for therapists. *Journal of Feminist Family Therapy: An International Forum, 24*(3), 272-289.

XV. Appendix A

MateMatch Questions

Directions: Relationship formation is a basic human drive, one that can lead to happiness, a sense of well-being, and even serve as a buffer against stress. While there are several articles and smartphone apps which offer suggestions of questions you can pose to your loved one, few are rooted in relationship science. MateMatch includes 14 questions to help you tackle some difficult topics with the hope of getting to know your significant other better. Take the time to answer these honestly. In addition, you will also be provided with the background research relating to each of these topics. The questions presented in this exercise can help couples understand what will and will not be tolerated by one another when in a relationship and will encourage them to have a conversation about both the present and the future. Be open, honest, ready to share, and ready to listen. Good luck!

Marisa T. Cohen, Ph.D.

Questions for Science of Relationships: MateMatch

1. **When describing your perfect mate, what are three qualities that you think are the most important?**
   Research has shown that individuals differ in the characteristics that they desire for a mate. However, we prefer people who are similar to ourselves. People also tend to prefer mates who are high in Agreeableness, Emotional Stability, and Intellect-Openness, and "having a mate low on these qualities [i]s linked in both sexes with marital and sexual unhappiness" (Botwin, Buss, & Shackelford, 1997, p. 133).

   Research has also shown strong evidence for assortative mating which involves the nonrandom coupling of individuals who resemble one another on one or more characteristics (Buss, 1984; Watson, Beer, & McDade-Montez, 2013).

2. **Should you set rules for your relationship? What boundaries do you feel are important for you to set between your partner and individuals of the opposite sex?**
   Research has shown that individuals overestimate agreement on rules and will often exhibit false confidence when it comes to knowledge of their partners (Roggensack & Sillars, 2014). Additionally, in their study of cheating and forgiveness, Gunderson and Ferrari (2008) note, "People are bound to violate their partners' expectations, which may disrupt the relationship and be deeply hurtful" (p.1).

3. **How much alone time is it important for you to have? Do you feel that it is important to spend all of your time with your partner or is it more important to maintain your space and personal identity?**
Research has shown that romantic relationships are a part of individuals' social experience and are linked to their relationships with their parents and peers (Connolly, 1996).

Debby Herbenick, Research Scientist and Co-Director of The Center for Sexual Health Promotion and a sexual health educator at The Kinsey Institute for Research in Sex, notes that if a person goes along with his/her partner's preferences when it comes to spending time together or alone, it can lead to frustration when their beliefs do not align. She says, "Being aware of your preferences means that you may be able to clarify your feelings about the relationship" (Herbenick, 2012).

4. **What are your views on gender roles? How will this affect the sharing of household roles and chores?**
Research has shown that women who make more money than men, spend more time on household chores. A reason for this is that they are trying to fit back in to their gender stereotypical role to compensate for making more than their male partner (Schneider, 2011).

5. **What are your views regarding finances? Do you feel that it is important to combine bank accounts or should each individual pay for his/her own purchases/expenses?**

   Financial issues are one of the biggest relationship stressors (Diamond & Hicks, 2011). Couples living together, but who were not currently married, were more likely to break up when there were financial disagreements (Dew, 2011).

6. **Do you and you partner share the same financial goals? In other words, is there a specific way in which you plan to save up for your future plans? Are you willing to compromise and/or negotiate those plans if they do not match with those of your partner?**

   According to previous research, financial satisfaction in a marital/long term relationship has a significant effect on the perception of relationship satisfaction. Tensions and disagreements over financial decisions reduce financial satisfaction, which can then have an effect on marital satisfaction (Archuleta, Grable, & Britt, 2013). Financial satisfaction can include individual assessments of debt, income, savings, and long-term goal achievement (Hira & Mugenda, 1999; Joo & Grable, 2004, as cited in Archuleta et al., 2013).

7. **Describe your ability to solve conflicts. When heated, do you like to handle issues as they arise, or is it more important to wait until you have calmed down before addressing any issues?**

   Conflict can be detrimental to the health of your relationship. Research has shown that feeling understood by your partner can serve as a buffer against the potentially detrimental effects of relationship conflict (Gordon & Chen, 2016).

8. **How important is having children to you?**

   Interviews with couples have shown that there are three different decision-making types when it comes to children: mutual early articulators, mutual postponers, and nonmutual couples. Mutual early articulator couples are those who make the decision early in the relationship not to have children, while mutual postponer couples are those who eventually agree not to have children, because neither member feels strongly about parenthood. Finally, nonmutual couples are those who draw out the process of arriving at a decision as to whether or not to have children, as the couple is mismatched. To avoid drawing out this process, it is best to have a frank discussion early on (Lee & Zvonkovie, 2014).

9. **How important are religion and spirituality to you?**

   Research has shown that higher levels of open communication about religion are associated with lower levels of relationship distress (Reiter & Gee, 2008).

10. Do you and your partner share the same political views? How confident are you that you and your partner will be able to "agree to disagree" on certain political matters?

A study was conducted with 51 heterosexual dating couples, in which data were collected at two different points, 11 months apart. Results demonstrated that "...intact couples differed less in their political and religious attitudes at study onset than did those who ended up dissolving" (Beske-Rechek, Remiker, & Baker, 2009, p. 151).

11. How was your relationship with your parents growing up?

Using a sample of 2,790 individuals from the National Longitudinal Study of Adolescent Health, researchers found that stronger parent-adolescent relationships predicted higher self-esteem during the transition to adulthood and higher intimate relationship quality (Johnson & Galambos, 2014).

12. Do you and your partner share the same overarching goals in life?

Avivi, Laurenceau, and Carver (2009) demonstrated that relationship quality positively relates to perceived goal sharing and perceived goal progress.

13. Do you and your partner know where each one of you stands in terms of sexual expectations?

Although there are various ways in which intimacy and love can be defined in a romantic relationship, research has shown that sexual satisfaction plays a major role in determining and maintaining relationship satisfaction. Researchers found that both the *quantity* as well as the *quality* of sexual activity between a married couple has a positive correlation with ratings of relationship quality/satisfaction (DeLamater, Hyde, & Frong, 2008; Parish et al., 2007).

14. How does your partner feel about owning pets?

Young adults and couples usually choose to raise a pet before children as a way to gain some experience. A study conducted by Allen (1995), revealed that couples who owned a dog were much more satisfied, and this increased as their attachment to their dogs increased. Studies have also shown that adding material constraints such as owning a pet increases the odds of a couple staying together by 10% (Walsh, 2009).

**These questions were taken from the MateMatch App.

Citation:

Cohen, M., & Dolma, D. (2016). MateMatch: A Relationship Primer. Retrieved from http://www.apple.com/ibooks/

MateMatch References

Allen, K. (1995). Coping with life changes and transitions: The role of pets. *Interactions, 13*(3), 5–8.

Archuleta, K. L., Grable, J. E., & Britt, S. L. (2013). Financial and relationship satisfaction as a function of harsh start-up and shared goals and values. *Journal of Financial Counseling and Planning, 24*(1), 3-14.

Avivi, Y. E., Laurenceau, J-P., & Carver, C. S. (2009). Linking relationship quality to perceived mutuality of relationship goals and perceived goal progress. *Journal of Social and Clinical Psychology, 28*, 137-164.

Bleske-Rechek, A., Remiker, M. W., & Baker, J. P. (2009). Similar from the start: Assortment in young adult dating couples and its link to relationship stability over time. *Individual Differences Research, 7*(3), 142-158.

Botwin, M. D., Buss, D. M, & Shackelford, T. K. (1997). Personality and mate preferences: Five factors in mate selection and marital satisfaction. *Journal of Personality, 65*(1), 107-136.

Buss, D. M. (1984). Marital assortment for personality dispositions: Assessment with three different data sources. *Behavior Genetics, 14*, 111–123.

Connolly, J. A., & Johnson, A. M. (1996). Adolescents' romantic relationships and the structure and quality of their close interpersonal ties. *Personal Relationships, 3*(2), 185-195.

DeLamater, J., Hyde, J. S., & Fong, M. (2008). Sexual satisfaction in the seventh decade of life. *Journal of Sex & Marital Therapy, 34*, 439-454.

Dew, J. (2011). Financial issues and relationship outcomes among cohabiting individuals. *Family Relations: An Interdisciplinary Journal of Applied Family Studies, 60*(2), 178-190.

Diamond, L. M., & Hicks, A. M. (2011). "It's the economy, honey!" Couples' blame attributions during the 2007-2009 economic crisis. *Personal Relationships, 19*(3), 586-600.

Gordon, A. M., & Chen, S. (2016). Do you get where I'm coming from? Perceived understanding buffers against the negative impact of conflict on relationship satisfaction. *Personality and Social Psychology, 110*(2), 239-260.

Gunderson, P., & Ferrari, J. (2008). Forgiveness of sexual cheating in romantic relationships: Effects of discovery method, frequency of offense, and presence of apology. *North American Journal of Psychology, 10*, 1–14.

Herbenick, D. (2012, December 17). Balancing time together vs. apart: Every relationship is a balance of time spent together and time spent alone. *Psychology Today*. Retrieved from https://www.psychologytoday.com/blog/the-pleasuressex/201212/balancing-time-together-vs-apart

Johnson, M. D., & Galambos, N. L. (2014). Paths to intimate relationship quality from parent-adolescent relations and mental health. *Journal of Marriage and Family, 76*(1), 145-160.

Lee, K., & Zvonkovie, A. M. (2014). Journeys to remain childless: A grounded theory examination of decision-making processes among voluntarily childless couples. *Journal of Social and Personal Relationships, 31*, 535-553. doi:10.1177/0265407514522891

Parish, W. L., Luo, Y., Stolzenberg, R. M., Laumann, E. O., Farrer, G., & Pan, S. (2007). Sexual practices and sexual satisfaction: A population based study of Chinese urban adults. *Archives of Sexual Behavior, 36*, 5–20.

Reiter, M. J., & Gee, C. B. (2008). Open communication and partner support in intercultural and interfaith romantic relationships: A relational maintenance approach. *Journal of Social and Personal Relationships, 25*(4), 539-559.

Roggensack, K. E., & Sillars, A. (2014). Agreement and understanding about honesty and deception rules in romantic relationships. *Journal of Social and Personal Relationships, 31*, 178-199.

Schneider, D. (2011). Market earnings and household work: New tests of gender performance theory. *Journal of Marriage and Family, 73*, 845-860.

Walsh, F. (2009). Human-animal bonds II: The role of pets in family systems and family therapy. *Family Process, 48*(4), 481-499.

Watson, D., Beer, A., & McDade-Montez, E. (2014). The role of active assortment in spousal similarity. *Journal of Personality, 82*(2), 116-129. doi:10.1111/jopy.12039

XVI. Acknowledgements

I would like to thank several people for making this book possible.

- To the team at ScienceofRelationships.com, thank you for your support, guidance, and welcoming me and my contributions.
- To the members of the Psychology Department at St. Francis College, for being such a wonderful source of support, on both a personal and professional level.
- To the SABL members (RAs and collaborators), who are not just students/former students, but colleagues and friends.
- To my parents, Linda and Bob, thank you for your unconditional love and support, and for instilling in me the belief that if I work hard and believe in myself, anything is possible.
- To Mike and Bisbee, for loving me more each and every day.

Marisa T. Cohen, Ph.D.

*Some of the chapters that appear in this book were originally published as articles for ScienceofRelationships.com

Made in the USA
Middletown, DE
11 April 2019